SIX-FIGURE
PET SITTING

*Catapult Your Pet Sitting Business
to Unlimited Success*

KRISTIN MORRISON
FOUNDER, SIX-FIGURE PET SITTING ACADEMY™

Six-Figure Pet Sitting: Catapult Your Pet Sitting Business to Unlimited Success
Copyright © 2010 by Kristin Morrison
All rights reserved.

ISBN: 978-0-615-43401-8

This book is dedicated to the hundreds of pet sitting business coaching clients in the United States and Canada with whom I've had the pleasure of coaching throughout the years. Thank you for trusting me to be your guide on your journey to business (and life) success. It's been an honor to witness the profound changes you've made in your businesses and in your personal lives.

— Kristin

Acknowledgments

Thank you to H.P. for your gentle and not-so-gentle nudging to write (and finally complete) this book.

I am especially grateful to my superb and loving team of pet sitting business managers, Melanie and Linda:

Thank you, Melanie. You have helped me in more ways than I can express, in business and in my life. Hiring you to manage my business restored my faith in letting go of the reins. I value your integrity and your competence. Thank you for being willing to be top dog while I travel for extended periods of 'soul travel.' I feel completely safe with you at the helm of the business. Thank you.

Thank you, Linda S., my angel-of-all-things! From weed-whacking and making sure my mail is picked up while I'm in Bali to managing my pet sitting business when Melanie is not working...is there anything you DON'T do? I think not. You also bring a smile to my face every time we talk. I didn't even know I needed a Linda S. until you walked into my life. Now I don't know what I would do without you.

And to my supportive family and friends and various locations that nurture me and helped me write this book:

Thank you, Dad, for always telling me I could do anything I want to do. I believe you!

Thank you, River, for reminding me that life is easy and fun. Your smile is so darn cute.

Thank you, Ann, for helping me edit this book so that I could finally complete it and offer it to pet sitters. I was concerned that the editing process would take away my 'voice' but you found it. Thank you so much.

Thanks, hiking trail on Gold Hill. You have been a place of deep inner restoration and a wellspring of creativity as I walk my path (literally and figuratively) each day.

Thank you to Bob, for reprimanding me when I didn't have a website those many years ago. I am grateful for your firm, direct, wise counsel that brought me to where I am today in my business and in my life. I thank you!

Thanks to Kathleena and Tarra, for your monthly support (and many phone calls) and for being a stand for all of my visions...including extended world travel and writing this book.

Thank you to Sharon, for being an example of a successful businesswoman who is committed to integrity. Your desire to create products that are earth-friendly, in spite of the potentially huge loss of profit to your company, brings tears to my eyes.

Thanks to my Thursday Afternoon Business Support Group, for all your guidance, love, connection and wisdom. I don't think my life and business would be as incredible as it is without you. In fact, I know it wouldn't.

Thanks to my beloved second home: Ubud, Bali. You have taught me much about myself, provided deep and utter relaxation and unfathomable mystery and magic. I felt this book stir inside me the last time I visited you. I look forward to our next adventure together.

Thanks to Susan, for showing me through your own writing process that authoring a book happens page-by-page, night-by-night (and sometimes weekend-by-weekend). Thank you also for being such a steadfast support and my Monday Record-Keeping Buddy since 2005!

Thank you to my Friday Night Girlfriends (Katie, Annie, Barb) who cheered me on with this and other business and personal projects throughout the years. I'm so very grateful for the constant, unwavering support and love I receive from you.

And though it is not often done…

Lastly, I thank myself for having the courage to live my dream in work and in play and for enjoying (most of) those evenings and sunny weekends I spent writing and completing this book.

Contents

Preface

Before we begin the journey to six-figures...

I wish I'd had this handbook when I started my pet sitting business in 1995! What you are holding is the culmination of my many years of learning the hard way – and often falling flat on my face – in order to realize what works and what doesn't when it comes to running a successful, six-figure pet sitting business.

I wrote this book so that you don't have to reinvent the wheel in terms of pet sitting business success. It is my intention that through these pages, you'll find your own mastery and six-figure profit in the world of professional pet sitting! Pet sitting is an exciting and fun business, and by applying what I've already learned, it can be a very lucrative and flexible one for you.

Although this book is primarily targeted to pet sitters who have already started their businesses, I am including some start-up information in Chapter 2 for those who need some business start-up tips. If you have already launched your pet sitting business, you can skip Chapter 2 or give it a quick review to ensure you haven't overlooked any important details.

I wish you much pet sitting business success!

Warmly,

Kristin Morrison
Founder, Six-Figure Pet Sitting Academy™

My Story

Before we begin *your* journey in the chapters that follow, I want to tell you about *my* story. In reading what I went through, I believe you'll quickly understand that my past business challenges are very similar to the ones you may be currently facing in your business. The lessons I learned the hard way are my inspiration for writing this book. In addition to being the owner of a large pet sitting and dog walking business based in California, I'm also a business coach for pet sitters and dog walkers and the founder of the Six-Figure Pet Sitting Academy™. However, I started out where, I suspect, you are now in your pet sitting business.

I began my pet sitting business in 1995 with the intention of running the business part-time while pursuing a 'real career.' After a year of part-time pet sitting, my business began to grow; I quit my day job, and opted to run the business as a full-time operation. When I started my pet sitting company, I knew nothing about running a business; I just knew I loved animals, and the business seemed like a good fit for me.

Like most of the pet sitters that I now coach, I made a lot of major mistakes along the way in almost all areas of my business including (but not limited to!): marketing, business and money management, hiring/firing, pricing, and the art of 'selling' my clients on our service... just to name a few. Initially, these mistakes were buoyed by my enthusiasm for my growing business, but after awhile, they began to negatively impact my business as well as affect my quality of life.

After a couple of years of running my business, I suddenly realized that I was working 12 to 14 hours a day, often seven days a week, and somehow not making a profit. As a pet sitter, can you relate to that? It was distressing, to say the least! The hectic work schedule and the responsibilities of owning my own business made me feel like I had a leash around my neck!

I also noticed that I was no longer simply 'Kristin Morrison.' Instead, I was 'Kristin Morrison, Business Owner.' I was pretty exhausted on a daily basis and almost entirely consumed by my business. I didn't have a life. Despite working so many hours a day, I wasn't even making a lot of extra money that I could really spend on myself. I was somehow only making enough to support my business. I couldn't understand how I was making so little money when I was working so many hours a day. It was ridiculous!

I also began eating on the run and eating the wrong food, and it seemed I was always eating in the car. I found I was getting massages all the time to compensate for the physical toll and stress I placed on my body due to working so hard. I didn't have time for my family and friends, so I began to feel pretty isolated. Plus, I didn't spend much quality time with my own pets and felt a bit neglectful of them. I felt like something had to give.

I began to think seriously about selling my pet sitting business, but something happened that completely altered the way I operated. I realized that, although I wanted to quit, I now had a taste of being self-employed, so the thought of working for someone else seemed impossible! Plus, I really loved animals and, though I was working long hours, I enjoyed having a job that paid me to work with cats and dogs.

I decided that I wanted to find a way to make my pet sitting business work *for* me instead of *against* me, so I decided to give myself ONE YEAR to make dramatic changes in the way I ran my business. I wanted to see if I could create a successful business defined by the things that mattered to me – having plenty of money and the time to do the things I like to do and enough space in each day to be with the people I love.

I decided that, if in one year my business began to generate a large profit and I started to feel more freedom, I would continue to run it. Freedom was an equally important consideration for me because there was no point to lots of money if there was no time to spend it and if my quality of life was poor.

So I committed to a solid year of doing everything I could think of to turn my business around. I decided that if the changes I made in one year's time didn't substantially raise my profits, in addition to giving me more time to just be 'me,' then I would opt to sell.

The race was on.

I became fearless and super creative about being open to and experimenting with new ways to run my pet sitting business. I felt like I had nothing to lose since I didn't want to run the business anymore… at least not the way I had been running it up until this point. Instead of me running my business, my business had been running me. In addition to exploring different ways to operate and manage staff members, I also began to educate myself about the nuts and bolts of really managing a solvent and successful business, including spread sheets, action steps to improve and expand each service we provided, search engine optimization research and marketing, just to name a few.

**MY GOAL:
IN ONE YEAR, IMPROVE
MY BUSINESS…
AND SUBSEQUENTLY MY
LIFE AND HAPPINESS…
OR SELL MY BUSINESS!**

Additionally, I also explored the psychology behind what my clients wanted and how I could best provide that for them. I learned the art of selling them on our great service without being pushy. (Yuck! Who wants pushy? Not me. And certainly not our clients.) These unique business practices and my ever-increasing business knowledge began to be reflected in my steadily rising profit margin, and more importantly for me, it was reflected in the ease with which I now managed my business.

Through this process of operating in an entirely different way, I began to realize that it wasn't the business that was creating a negative effect on my life; it was the way I ran my business. As I made the changes within my business, I began to enjoy my life more. I began to smile more. I felt like I had a life again! And the money that was now coming in, in an easy and nearly effortless way, didn't hurt either. After that one year I checked the numbers: I'd made more money in that single year than in the previous two years combined!

More importantly was the ease with which I now managed my business. These changes were also reflected in the fact that, for the first time since starting my business, I had time to myself again.

I was now 'Kristin Morrison' for more of each week than I was 'Kristin Morrison, Business Owner.' I began to breathe more deeply. I began to notice I was enjoying life more. The positive changes that I made in my business in that one year also began to positively affect nearly every single area of my life. I felt personally renewed and transformed because of the transformation in my business.

This book was written to give you step-by-step instructions and share what I did in that year to create the highly successful pet sitting business that I still run today. Recognizing a lack of business education for pet sitters and also realizing that a lot of pet sitters were running their non-traditional businesses in traditional ways, I began providing out-of-the-box business coaching for those pet sitters struggling in their businesses. A lot of the exercises that I've used with my coaching clients are in this book.

Through this book, one-on-one telephone coaching, teleclasses, webinars, and business products targeted for the pet sitting business owner, the Six-Figure Pet Sitting Academy™ teaches pet sitters the necessary business skills and some unusual management techniques that are guaranteed to dramatically raise profits.

I continue to run my California-based pet sitting company, which currently has 35 staff members, two managers and over 750 active clients. Even though my pet sitting company profits continue to grow annually, my work hours have been dramatically reduced since I changed the way I run my business: I now work only three or four days a week.

Through this book and the programs offered at the Six-Figure Pet Sitting Academy™, it is my intention to give pet sitters a solid road map to creating their own successful businesses that is easy to operate and profitable. Care to join me?

Then please, read on.

ONE

Charting Your Course:

Creating the Foundation to Build a Six-Figure Pet Sitting Business

"Whenever you see a successful business, someone once made a courageous decision."

–Peter Drucker

If you are reading this book, then you probably want your business to be more successful than it currently is, and I'll guess that you obviously want to make more money than you are currently making. So congratulations for taking that first step toward making six-figures in your pet sitting business!

Pain or discomfort is often the main motivator for change. Pain propels us to take action as human beings. If you weren't in pain in your business, then you probably wouldn't be inspired to grow. In that regard, if you are experiencing a lack of money or knowledge about running a successful business, consider it a gift. Why? Because that pain or financial lack will help get you to where you want to be – running a successful, six-figure pet sitting company.

Money is not the answer to everything, nor does it buy happiness. However, having more money does enable us to have more freedom and a sense of control over our lives. I truly believe that if I can create a six-figure pet sitting business then anyone can, including you! I never imagined that I would grow to actually love being a businesswoman and a successful one at that, especially because of my dislike for math in any way, shape or form when I was growing up....and obviously running a successful business requires math skills.

What I did have, which is perhaps what you have, was the willingness to do whatever it took to create the pet sitting business of my dreams. I was not willing to invest years and years in the process of discovering how to be successful. I had neither the time nor the energy for that. Instead I was willing to commit a single year and dedicate myself entirely to my goal of creating a six-figure pet sitting business.

PAIN IS THE MOTIVATOR TO CHANGE. NO ONE LIKES IT, BUT IT IS THE IMPETUS OFTEN NEEDED TO TAKE THE STEPS TOWARD GROWTH.

That's right: one year. 365 days.

If *you* want to create a six-figure pet sitting business, then what I ask from you is that you follow the instructions exactly as I've outlined and explained them in this book. *You will reap results and high profits* from this information if you do exactly what I'm about to share for an entire year.

Even if your service area is saturated with pet sitters and you face considerable competition, you can still achieve six-figure results in your business. How? Because you will be running your business in a distinctly different way than any other pet sitter in your area.

Are you ready to explore how YOU can create a six-figure pet sitting business? If so, let's begin.

How to Use this Book

In the chapters to follow, you will occasionally see a *Six-Figure Success Tip*. These tips were written to give you an extra boost toward your goal of making six-figures. Pay special attention to them and watch your profits rise!

At the end of each chapter, there will be 'Action Steps' for you to do. These action steps will create mastery in each area where you want and need more business success. You are now on your way to six-figure pet sitting success, and I look forward to being your guide through the very same process that led to my continued success in my own business, regardless of the amount of competition or the state of the economy!

So let's begin with the first of the action steps you'll find throughout this book:

Action Step

Purchase a timer and keep it in your office. I've found timers to be incredibly helpful to stay on track and to stay intentional in taking action on business tasks. I'll be referring to exercises that include a timer throughout this book, so make it a point to get one as soon as possible.

Action Step

Purchase a journal to complete the exercises in this book. Having the written portion of your journey to six-figures in one spot will enable you to chart your progress, and a year from now, you'll be able to see how far you've come!

Action Step

Where are you currently feeling the most pain or discomfort in your business? If you haven't yet started a business, then notice where you are feeling pain or discomfort in your financial situation or your current career. Write at least a page on what the discomfort is and what you think could remedy it. Don't worry about grammar or punctuation. The importance of this exercise is to make you really focus on exactly what your pain point is in your business and how you might alleviate it.

TWO

Getting Started:

12 Start-up Tips to Ensure Business Success from the Beginning

*"The beginning is the
most important part of the work."*

–Plato

As I mentioned, I've written this book to help those who have already launched their pet sitting businesses turn them into six-figure enterprises. However, I realize some of you might be at the beginning of the venture or still considering making the leap. For those of you in that situation, this chapter is specifically for you. I'll be sharing the reasons to consider launching and operating a pet sitting business as well as a dozen start-up tips to help you avoid making the mistakes I did when I began.

If you've already started your business, I certainly encourage you to give this chapter a quick read anyway to help you ensure that you've taken the initial steps correctly, have all of your "i's dotted and t's crossed" and have a solid foundation in place.

First and foremost, it's important to understand that pet sitting is a real business and provides you with a real opportunity to earn six-figures. A lot of people think of pet sitting as a hobby-type business, and while it can start that way, if you follow the advice I share in this book, it can become a powerful, sustainable business.

And if you're struggling like I was, feeling like the leash is around your neck, you'll find if you change the way you run your business, you will change your life as well.

Secondly, a new business is like an infant. It needs your nurturing and attention at the beginning in order to stand on its own and to grow. Just as an infant grows and becomes more independent each week, month and year, so will your business if you nurture it. The information I'm going to share with you will help expedite that process. Remember, I want you to avoid all the mistakes I made in the beginning.

5 Reasons to Start a Pet Sitting Business

It's an exciting time to start a pet sitting business. Even when consumers fret over the economy, the pet industry continues to thrive. Pet owners do not hesitate to spend money on their pets.

The pet industry encompasses everything from veterinary services and pet food to pet sitting and dog walking. This industry is expected to generate over $50 billion (yes, that's billion with a B) annually, and it's trending up, according to industry research firm IBISWorld. Trust me; there are enough dogs and cats to go around to keep all of us pet sitters busy... and earning real income. It's estimated that one-third of all homes in America have a pet. In the past, many pet owners would rely on family or neighbors to pet sit; however, more and more people live farther from family members and many don't even know their neighbors.

If you are considering starting a pet sitting business, here are the top five reasons to motivate you to actually take the actions necessary to start your business now:

Reason #1:

A pet sitting business lets you begin while maintaining your current job or career. Remember my analogy of a new business being like a baby? Keeping your day job gives you time to nurture your business the same way you'd nurture your infant. You certainly wouldn't expect an infant to be able to support you, would you? Of course not, and your business won't fully support you at first either.

Because the hours of pet sitting visits can be somewhat flexible (generally 6 to 9 a.m. and 6 to 9 p.m.), you can work your business hours around your current job. This will help you ease your way into your new pet sitting business to see if you would like to make a full-time job of it. Pet sitting is one of the rare businesses that enables you to work a somewhat flexible schedule.

Reason #2:

Pet sitting business start-up costs are as low as $1,500 or less. Since you will be providing care in the pets' homes, you will not have to rent a place of business, and you can do office work from your own home.

Start-up costs include:

- Marketing materials: logo, business cards, website, and some other forms of advertising.
- Pet sitting forms, contracts, and agreements which you can find at: http://www.sixfigurepetsittingacademy.com/petsitter_products.html.
- Pet supplies: leashes, dog barrier / gate for your car, pet first aid kit in your car, fanny pack, poop bags, mace or pepper spray, dog treats.
- Business phone line.
- Membership in a national pet sitting business association.
- Insurance and bonding.

Reason #3:

You can get paid to exercise. There are very few jobs out there that enable you to get paid to walk in the fresh air and burn calories while making money, but pet sitting is one of them! Walking dogs is a necessary aspect to the pet visits that you will be doing, and most pet sitters really enjoy this aspect of the business: Paid exercise!

Reason #4:

Pet sitting is a lucrative profession. Pet owners love their 'kids' and are generally willing to pay their pet sitters well for quality pet care. Though 'hobby pet sitters' usually charge substantially lower rates for their pet care services, professional pet sitters with insurance can charge enough to earn a very lucrative income. As I've said, pet sitting is a real business and one in which you truly can earn six-figures.

Reason #5:

You get paid to work with animals! Working with dogs, cats and other animals is incredibly rewarding. Day after day, you will receive unconditional love and adoration from loving pets. Where else can you get that kind of adoration at your job?

So now that you understand the top reasons to begin a pet sitting business, let's look at 12 simple steps to build a solid foundation for a real business. If you've already started your business, I strongly suggest a quick review here to make certain you haven't missed any of these critical steps.

12 Simple Start-up Tips for New Pet Sitters

☑ **Step #1:** Choose a business name that you LOVE.

Naming a business is as important as naming your kid. Maybe even more important! Why? Because your child can change his name eventually if he wants to, but trying to change a business name down the road is a *very* challenging process. (I changed my business name after a year, so I'm speaking from experience.)

I recommend that you pick a name that you can see yourself using ten or twenty years down the road. Presume you'll be in business that long.

Don't call your business "Bakerville Pet Sitting" (or something similar) if you have even the slightest inkling to perhaps expand to the surrounding areas. You'll be stuck in Bakerville! However, if you are really clear that you want to stay small, then go for it. It's actually a nice name. But you must understand how that sort of name brands you to a specific location. If you're uncertain about how you envision the future of your business, I'd avoid such a localized name.

SIX-FIGURE SUCCESS TIP

Do as much online searching as you can before committing to a business name. You want to ensure that you are not 'taking' another local company's name. Check your local phone book and do Internet searches.

If you find that no one in your county is using the name that you've selected, then it may be yours to use in your area. If you discover that the business name is being used in another city or state, contact your local city hall to ask about the laws regarding name usage.

If you think that you may want to create more branches of your company in other counties, I highly recommend that you do a name search at the U.S. Patent and Trademark website at: http://www.uspto.gov.

Make certain there is no trademark on the name you are interested in. If there is, it's best to pick another name, so that you are not 'stealing' someone else's name and facing possible legal action from that same-named company in the future. Doing your homework now will save you a lot of time, money, and frustration in the future.

Do describe your service in your business name. I don't recommend "pet care" – it's too vague. But "pet sitting and dog walking" are great to add: Bakerville Pet Sitting and Dog Walking Service. Some may find it's a bit long, but, in my opinion, better too long than not descriptive enough. This way, clients will know exactly what you do. And with a descriptive name, you're already on your way to optimizing for search engines. (More on that in another chapter.)

☑ Step #2: Get a Business License / Fictitious Business Name (DBA)

Now that you have your name, the next step on the agenda is getting a business license.

Before you get your business license, you'll have to decide if you want to be a sole proprietor, an LLC (Limited Liability Corporation) or a Corporation. This is an important decision. Check with your accountant to find out which type of business structure is best for you.

A sole proprietorship is a business formation in which you own all of the assets of your business as well as all of the profits it generates. It is the least expensive to organize, and you retain complete control. However, you also assume all the business risk, liabilities and debts. There is no separation between your personal and business funds.

A corporation, on the other hand, is its own legal entity. Shareholders (in this case, you) have limited liability for debts and judgments against the company. Your personal bank account remains separate from the company's money. The downside is that corporations are cumbersome and expensive to form, and they may result in higher taxes overall.

An LLC, or limited liability corporation, is a bit of a hybrid between the first two. It combines the ability to control your fiscal liabilities in the company (i.e. creating a protective firewall between the company's money and your personal savings) while maintaining more flexibility and control like a sole proprietorship. It's more expensive to create than a sole proprietorship, and LLCs are not permissible in all states.

With the help of your accountant, once you've decided what category of business you'd like to create, you are now ready to get a business license.

In some cities, you may have to get a county business license and a city business license if you are providing pet sitting for different cities within your county while also working from your home office. Call your local City Hall to find out how and where to get your business license. Also, be clear when applying that you are not maintaining animals on your property as a commercial venture (unless you are providing dog boarding in your home as one of your services).

A fictitious business name, sometimes called fictitious title or DBA, may be required. If you are named Jerry and your business is called Jerry's Pet Sitting Service, you will not need to get a fictitious business name. However, if your name is Amanda and you want to name your business "Jerry's Pet Sitting" or if you want to do business as "Bakerville Pet Sitting and Dog Walking," then you will need to get a fictitious business name. Why? Because your name is not part of your legal business name, and city and state laws require that all businesses that don't have the owner's name in them get this special fictitious title, so that the city and state can determine exactly who the owner is. Once again, your accountant and/or your local government can offer some advice about whether or not you will need to apply for and obtain a fictitious title.

☑ **Step #3:** Purchase necessary forms and contracts for your business

Next you'll want to get forms and contracts for your business. You'll find many to choose from online. The Six-Figure Pet Sitting Academy™ has a Business Start-up Kit for Pet Sitters™ as well as individual forms and contracts that you can purchase online.

You can find them at:

http://www.sixfigurepetsittingacademy.com/petsitter_products. html

You can instead create your own forms if you'd prefer. You don't need to buy forms, but it does save a lot of time and eliminates your need to reinvent the wheel.

Here are all the business forms you'll want to have ready before you take on your first client:

- Client Interview/Intake Form for Pet Sit Clients (for Overnights and Visits)
- Client Interview/Intake Form for Dog Walk Clients
- Client Questionnaire for Feedback from Clients
- Checklist for Overnight Pet Sitting Jobs
- Checklist for Pet Visit Jobs
- Contract for Pet Sitting Clients
- Contract for Dog Walking Clients
- Veterinary Release Agreement
- Key Release Agreement

☑ **Step #4:** Get a business-only phone number.

Do NOT give out your cell phone to clients! I know that when you are starting out, you don't want to miss a call or an opportunity; however, I have worked with so many coaching clients who made that mistake and now, years later, are stressed out because their pet sitting clients call them at all hours. Now they are struggling to have a life! Giving clients your cell phone number now is the same as putting a leash around YOUR neck and keeping it on... and then your clients get to pull it whenever they want. Don't do it. It's inexpensive to get a separate business number, so there are no excuses for you to put that leash around your neck.

You DO want to answer your business phone directly as often as possible, especially when you are starting out. Your clients and prospects will have more confidence in you if you're truly available rather than being directed to voice mail. It's good customer service. You can have your business line forwarded to your cell phone to help ensure you can field as many calls as possible. However, if you do this, make sure that you have a blocked or private number on your cell phone. Otherwise, clients will see your number on their Caller ID and inevitably call you back on your cell phone, and you've lost your ability to have a break from your business when you need it.

Google Voice is another great option. It's free, and you can direct calls to your cell, your home and to voice mail. In fact, you can route <u>all</u> of your phone numbers through Google Voice, and you establish the rules regarding how each call is directed.

☑ Step #5: Decide what type of animals to care for and services to offer.

Decide what types of animals you'll care for so that you can then get clear on what services you will offer those types of animal.

Dogs and cats are standard, and some pet sitters also care for horses and other farm animals, as well as reptiles, rabbits, birds, fish, and pocket pets (mice and hamsters). Decide what animals you will feel most comfortable caring for.

Here are the standard services that most pet sitters offer for dogs, cats and other household pets:

- Private or small group dog walking
- Group dog hiking, dog park adventures, or beach playtime
- Vacation pet visits

- Overnight pet sitting in client's home
- Dog boarding in pet sitter's home
- Pet taxi

Here's a breakdown of the service description, typical time commitment and time of day the service usually takes place:

Private or Group Dog Walking

What the service is: Neighborhood dog walking

Time commitment: 30/45/60 minutes

Time of day service takes place: usually mid-day hours of 11-2

Group dog hiking, dog park adventure, or beach playtime:

What service is: Social and active playtime for dogs

Time commitment: play/walk time of 45/60 minutes plus drive time to and from beach or trail (2-4 hours total)

Time of day service takes place: usually mid-day hours of 11-2

Vacation Pet Visits

What the service is: For pets: feeding, walking, administering medication if necessary, scooping the litter box and cleaning up any messes pets may have made while human clients are away. For home: watering plants, retrieving mail and newspaper, adjusting blinds and turning on lights at night to give a "lived-in" appearance to home.

Time commitment: 30/45/60 minutes, 2 or 3 times a day

Time of day service takes place: 7-9am, 11am-2pm, 7-9pm (Every 12 hours if 2x daily visits, every 8 hours if 3x a day visits)

Overnight Pet Sitting in Client's Home

What the service is: For pets: feeding and walking, administering medication if necessary, scooping the litter box and cleaning up any messes pets may have made while human clients are away. For home: watering plants and retrieving mail and newspaper, adjusting blinds and turning on lights at night to give a "lived-in" appearance to home, and staying overnight in the home.

Time commitment: usually 12 hours overnight with a mid-day visits if needed.

Time of day service takes place: usually 7pm-7am with a 30 or 45 minute mid-day visit/walk between 11am-2pm if needed.

Dog Boarding in Pet Sitter's Home

What the service is: Keeping the dog at your home or at one of your staff member's homes.

Time commitment: Depends upon dogs' and clients' needs. With some dogs, you may need to take them with you wherever you go due to separation anxiety.

Time of day service takes place: 24-hour care.

Pet Taxi

What the service is: Transporting the animal(s) to and from their homes to the specified destination, usually the veterinarian or dog groomer.

Time Commitment: Depends upon dogs' and clients' needs, usually a minimum of an hour to and from the destination.

Time of day service takes place: Whatever time client specifies.

☑ Step #6: Figure out your pricing for each pet service you offer.

Are you confused about how to price your various pet services? Do an online search for the various pet sitting services in your area. You'll read more about pricing in a further chapter, but when you're starting out, I recommend positioning yourself in the middle of the average rates in your area – not the highest, not the lowest, but right in the middle. If you've been pet sitting for a year or longer, then go with the high-medium to low-high pricing for your locale.

Create a pricing spreadsheet for all of your various services. Post it where you can see it, so that when clients call, you will know immediately how to respond. Do role-playing sessions with friends and have them call you to ask for pricing for different assortments of animals. Have them rate you on how confident, trustworthy and personable you came across on the phone.

As your business increases (and even if your business is relatively new), you can raise your prices to the high-medium or low-high range as you see fit. Let clients know you have space for more business. Reward them with a free dog walk or pet sit visit if they refer you to new clients.

☑ Step #7: Join a pet sitting association.

You'll want to become a member of a national pet sitting association. Why? The most important reason I've found to join an association is to get a lower rate for business insurance. You can take advantage of the group policy that associations offer. You'll also have the opportunity to get discounts on other business items as well as use of the association as a valuable resource to answer any questions you might have about pet sitting or general start-up questions.

I've found that all of the pet sitting associations are excellent in their own ways, and my own personal experience is that the National Association of Professional Pet Sitters (NAPPS) offers valuable business information for pet sitting business owners. I'm committed to helping pet sitters become knowledgeable about how to run a business, not just how to take care of pets, and I find NAPPS excels in the area of business and pet care education. Please note that there is a yearly membership fee to join, but this more than pays for itself with the substantial discount that you will receive on business insurance as well as the other perks that that come with being a member.

Here is the NAPPS website: http://www.petsitters.org.

☑ Step #8: Obtain Business Insurance.

You can get pet sitting business insurance on a shoestring. If you don't have enough money in your start-up budget to purchase a membership to an association, yet you still want low-cost business insurance, I recommend Pet Sit, LLC. They offer inexpensive insurance without paying a yearly membership association fee.

You can find Pet Sit, LLC online at: http://www.petsitllc.com.

If you have many staff members or are considering hiring staff members this year, then I recommend that you compare prices and make sure that Pet Sit, LLC is the most cost-effective way of obtaining insurance. You may end up paying more for insurance if you have many staff members than you would if you joined an association and purchased business insurance through your organization's insurance plan. However, if you are a sole proprietor or have just a handful of staff members, then Pet Sit, LLC can definitely get you insured quickly and inexpensively so you can say "yes" to your first client!

☑ Step #9: Get Bonded.

In addition to being responsible for your clients' pets, you will also be responsible for their property. I get a lot of calls from pet sitters asking me if they should get bonded (anti-theft insurance) since they are a sole proprietor, and they know they will not be stealing from their clients. Yes, you should get it. Why? It's inexpensive, and you can get a policy for as little as $75 annually. Clients will appreciate knowing you are bonded. Also having Licensed/ Bonded/Insured on your business card and on your website really shows your professionalism. Do it!

You can purchase bonding insurance through the same insurance company that is offered by NAPPS or you can get it through Pet Sit, LLC.

☑ Step #10: Issue a press release.

You'll want to send out press releases to your local newspapers. It's a good idea to both e-mail and snail mail it. While you want to toot your own horn, remember that press releases announce news. Stick to the facts, and there's a better chance that your local newspapers will print your release. Don't forget to include some quotations, even if you're quoting yourself. If you get too "salesy," they're bound to ignore it.

Find out who the business editors for your local newspaper (or papers if you are covering a larger geographic area) are and send your release to their attention. Various publications may also offer submission guidelines. Find them online or ask for them and be certain you adhere to them. Your press release will likely end up in the trash if you fail to follow the submission guidelines.

Here's a sample to give you an idea:

For immediate release:

New Pet Sitting Service Announced
Bakerville, VA, October 25, 2010

Pet-care specialist, Jenny Smith, has announced the opening of the Bakerfield Pet Sitting Service, serving Bakerfield and surrounding communities. Ms Smith has over fifteen years of pet care experience for friends and family.

When asked about the importance of pet sitting services, she explained, "Staying in a kennel is often more stressful to pets than their owners realize. With my service, pets can be cared for in the comfort of their own homes – the surroundings they know best."

Before relocating to Bakerfield, Ms Smith previously lived in Atlanta where she volunteered for the Atlanta Animal Shelter for fifteen years. She decided to launch her business to provide a much-needed service in this community and to pursue her passion for working with animals.

Walking and feeding pets during owner absences is the primary function of her business, and she also provides pet transportation and dog park visits. Additionally, her service is not limited to dogs and cats. "While dogs and cats make up the bulk of our clientele, we also provide care for horses, goats, chickens, bunnies, birds and pocket pets," she added.

In addition to providing in-home care for pets, the Bakerfield Pet Service also offers boarding in a home atmosphere.

For additional information, call at 809-421-9567 or visit online at http://www.bakervillepetsitting.com.

#

Contact:
Jenny Smith, Owner, Bakerfield Pet Siting
2809 Magnolia Drive
Bakerfield, VA 22901
Phone: 809-421-9567

http://www.bakervillepetsitting.com
info@bakervillepetsitting.com

Be certain to end your press release professionally by typing a series of pound signs (# # #) instead of using the phrase "the end" and provide full contact details so the reporter can contact you with questions or for further information.

In addition to your press release, there are a number of other aspects of marketing that are crucial to operate a successful six-figure pet sitting business. We'll delve into those later in the book. For now, here's the list to consider:

✓ Professional logo

✓ Business cards

✓ Website domain name (URL)

✓ Website

✓ Search Engine Optimization (SEO) for your website

✓ Pay-per-click advertising

✓ Pet sitting directory listings

✓ Social media sites: Twitter, Facebook, LinkedIn, etc.

✓ Blogs and articles (creates high SEO for websites)

☑ Step #11: Develop a business plan.

Having a business goal is great, but it's not worth very much if you don't have a plan to achieve it. Developing a business plan creates the map you need to get where you know you want to go – reaching a six-figure pet sitting business. A business plan is a formal statement about your business goals and how to go about achieving them. It includes a description of your business, your background and experience, a competitive analysis, your marketing plan, and your plans for running your operation.

Some new entrepreneurs see writing a business plan as little more than busywork; however, it forces you to really think about these important aspects of running your business. As you grow, your plan can grow with you. Additionally, when you grow to the point of considering outside funding, a business plan will be required by almost all lenders.

I'll cover how you can create a simple, quick business plan in the next chapter.

☑ Step #12: Get administration software.

One of the keys to running a successful, six-figure pet sitting business is to *run the business* rather than letting *your business run you*. One of the most important items for your new business is a software system that allows you to easily invoice clients, keep track of your client, pet, and staff information, and to maintain your pet sitting and dog walking schedule.

With the advances in online security and flexibility, I highly recommend using an online administration software system rather than a stand-alone one. The reason is simple: It enables you to manage your business from anywhere in the world. Plus it allows your managers (when you eventually grow your business and need them) to control every aspect of the business from their own homes.

This type of system may involve a monthly or annual fee that is usually based on the number of users. The more staff you have, the more expensive it becomes. However, this fee will pay for itself several times over with the level of flexibility you get and the ease with which you can run your business! Before you opt for a particular system, envision what you want your business to become and choose the system that supports that vision. It's easier to grow into a system that offers more features than you may need when you start than to change administrative systems down the road.

There are many software systems available for pet sitters. To find the one that works best for you and your business, Google "pet sitting software systems" or "pet sitting administration software."

Action Step

Notice which of the 12 business start-up steps above you have completed, and which ones still need to be finished. Chart out what still needs to be completed in your start-up phase with free "mind mapping" software which will help you clearly define what you need to do next. You can choose the mind mapping software that works best for you by reviewing the following website:

http://en.wikipedia.org/wiki/List_of_mind_mapping_software

THREE

The One-Hour Business Plan:

Planning Your Work, Working Your Plan

*"Your plan is a compass.
It will always tell you where to go next."*

–Oleg Vishnepolsky,
Chief Technology Officer
for 24/7 Real Media

Whether you are just getting started in your pet sitting business or have owned your business for years, it's crucial to create a business plan. A business plan is a map for business owners, and by completing a business plan, you will get clarity on where you want to go and how best to get there.

Some business owners take the time to complete a business plan, file it away and rarely, if ever, refer to it again. As I said, your business plan is your map. Would you embark on a long drive to a new destination without a map (forget about GPS and other electronic helpers for the moment)? Probably not. Now what would happen if you reviewed your map the night before you left, shoved in the glove compartment and did not refer to it again during your journey? Would you end up where you wanted to go? Probably not, or you might manage to get there after a lot of wrong turns, wasted time and wasted money. The same thing is true of your business plan. Review it regularly to make certain you stay on track to reach your goal – your six-figure pet sitting business.

Sometimes along the way, you may find another route or change your mind about your destination. The same thing can happen as your business grows. However, don't change course without updating your business plan as well.

In addition to serving as your map, your business plan also spells out your vision and your approach to others. If you have any thoughts about obtaining a loan or funding, or attracting investors, a business plan is a must.

One of the aspects of your business plan is market analysis. I encourage you not to gloss over this. It will help you define what you truly want to do and how much demand there is for your service. Some questions to think about while you are completing this section are:

- What is the demographic of your average customer?
- Do they live in an area you would like to service?
- Is their income high enough to warrant hiring you?
- What type of customers are you most comfortable with?
- Do you want to specialize in a particular breed?
- Do you want to exclude particular breeds or types of pets?
- What services do you want to include or exclude?

Below is a simple business plan that you can complete in less than an hour which will help get you started on the road to creating the business of your dreams.

Action Step

Set your timer for one hour and get out your journal and complete the following worksheet:

The One Hour Business Plan

Business name: _____

Owner(s): _____

Type of ownership:

- ❏ *Sole Ownership*
- ❏ *Partnership*
- ❏ *Corporation*

Type of business:

_____

_____

Employees/Independent Contractors: (including owner):

Full time: _____   *Part-time:* _____

History of your business:
(When you started, and your business experience background)

_____

_____

_____

Business overview

A. Why do you think your pet sitting business will be successful?

_____

_____

_____

B. How do you sell your service?

_____

_____

_____

*C. Promotion/advertising (Explain your company's advertising policy
and marketing activities):*

_____

_____

_____

D. Services you provide:

_____

_____

_____

Identify competition

(Who is your competition and where are they located?)

_____

_____

_____

_____

_____

_____

Market analysis

(Describe your average customer & from what areas you draw your customers)

_____

_____

_____

_____

_____

_____

_____

Future Plans

• Short range goals (6-12 months)

_____

_____

• Long range goals (2-5 years)

_____

_____

FOUR

Because You're Worth It:

How Commitment and Self-Worth
Lead to Net Worth

"Reality forms around commitment."

–Anonymous

As I mentioned earlier, pain or discomfort is usually the motivator for change. In fact, it's typically a stronger motivator than happiness. People will act quicker to eliminate pain than to create happiness. If you weren't in pain in your business right now, you probably wouldn't be reading this book. If you're thinking of launching a pet-sitting business, you may be reading this book to avoid *potential* business pains. Either way, pain is not necessarily a bad thing. It forces change. Change propels us forward as human beings and as business owners. Without change, there is no growth.

I also said earlier that money is not the answer to everything, but financial security brings with it a sense of freedom and control over your life. Numerous studies on happiness have shown that having a sense of control over our lives and in our work brings happiness. Greater financial security means greater control. That control may or may not bring you happiness. It did for me.

As I shared with you in my story, I never imagined that I would grow to love running a business, and a successful one at that, because I always equated running a business with a lot of math, and

I disliked math. But what I had was the desire to be successful and create a lucrative pet sitting business. You are reading this book, so you probably share that desire.

The first key to creating a successful business is to define what having a successful business would look like for YOU.

ONLY YOU CAN DEFINE YOUR OWN SUCCESS. WHAT'S IMPORTANT TO ME MAY NOT BE IMPORTANT TO YOU. YOU DEFINE IT.

Each person's definition of success is different. As *you* begin to get focused on creating success in your own pet sitting business, it's important to outline your personal view of what that success looks like. Not for anyone else but for you. Now my definition of business success after having my pet sitting business since 1995 may be shocking to some of you, and to others, maybe not so much.

Here's my definition of business success based on where I am in relationship to my business <u>now</u>:

- Making over six-figure's net profit.
- Working three to four days a week (15-25 hours per week).
- Working *on* my business more than I work *in* my business.
- Having the ability to travel for four out of every twelve months.

I know to some of you that may sound outrageous. I never could have imagined that I could create that kind of lifestyle for myself, but I have. I didn't start out with that definition of success, but I've grown into that as my business has grown and prospered.

Initially my definition of success was simply to be able to make ends meet each month. That may be where you are now. Or your definition of success might be to have time off on the weekends. And that's fine; however, it's important to also have big-picture goals in addition to the smaller ones – to think about what you want for yourself and your business in a few years even if it seems impossible now.

It's important to start out by assessing where your business is now, and by starting with smaller goals, you can take your business in the direction you want to go. Setting smaller goals initially makes your big-picture goals more attainable. It becomes manageable, and bite-sized chunks give you successes along the way, putting you on the right path to your ultimate dream. Remember, I started out defining success as making ends meet and having a little time off now and then. That bite-sized goal put me on the path to the current definition of success that I'm enjoying.

What is *your* definition of your own business success for this year? What would that success look like for you? Keep it simple and be specific:

- A 5-day workweek.
- Making $70,000 this year.
- Doing only mid-day and evening pet visits (no morning pet visits).

Jot these thoughts down in your journal as they come to you. But don't write them down and forget about them. Be sure to review them on a weekly or monthly basis or post them where you can see them daily in your office so that your vision of success stays front and center.

You don't have to know how you will achieve these definitions of success – that will come in later chapters. For now, simply allow yourself to dream about where you want to go.

The second key to creating a successful business is being 100% committed to your business success.

When I started to become serious about creating a successful business, I realized I was not willing to invest years and years to discover how to be successful. I had neither the time nor the energy for that. Also, my finances wouldn't allow me to waste time on methods that didn't work to create success. I needed to make money in my business, good money... soon... or I was going to have to quit and do something else.

As I mentioned in my story, I was working 12- to 14-hour days, was totally exhausted and was on the verge of selling my business. I could not bear the thought of working as hard as I had been working for another day. And if I thought I had to work like that for the rest of my life, I would not have been willing to do it. No way. Perhaps you feel the same way. But what if you knew *in advance* that working 12- to 14-hours a day for one year would result in doubling your profit? What if you knew that eventually you'd be working far fewer hours? In fact, what if you knew you'd be working less than half of what you do now? Would you be willing to commit to working hard for such a positive result? Absolutely. That is exactly what I did. And you can too.

Here's the thing: I'm not here to give you a get-rich-quick scheme. In the business of pet sitting, as with any business, you can't make money without investing a bit of money and time. The return on your investment is that eventually (if you run your business in the way I outline in this book) you'll have a lot more of both! So be willing to work hard for *one year*. By working hard, I mean actually doing the steps listed in this book. If you knew that you could work hard for one year and then work the schedule of your dreams for the next ten years, would you do it? I bet you *are* willing to work hard because you were willing to purchase this book, and you are now reading this book with the intention to create a six-figure pet sitting business.

ONE YEAR OF HARD WORK AND EFFORT CAN RESULT IN LIVING YOUR DREAM. MAKE THE COMMITMENT, AND YOU WON'T REGRET IT.

As I also shared in my story, I decided to commit to my business for one year and give myself entirely to my goal of creating a successful pet sitting business in that year. I made a commitment that, even when I didn't want to, I would market my business. Even when I was tired, I would take that extra client. Even when I didn't want to, I would hire another person to help me because I realized I couldn't take on additional work if I had to do it all myself.

Make a commitment to yourself that from this date forward you will give yourself *an entire year* to work as hard as you can. You will invest as much of yourself as you can muster in the next year through the exercises in this book and your own tenacity to really make your dreams of making more money and having a better business come true. Can you do that?

If so, let your spouse or partner know or call up a trusted friend right now and verbally declare that you are willing to give your business all of you, so that you can make more money and eventually have more time off. One of the most powerful actions you can take in your business starting today is to commit to doing *whatever it takes* to have your business be successful. When I say fully commit, I mean to make a declaration to yourself as well as to someone that you know and trust. Say out loud that you are willing to do what you can to make your business successful.

SIX-FIGURE SUCCESS TIP

Did you read the acknowledgement section of this book? If so, you read the names of the people and organizations that were supportive and often instrumental in the writing of this book you are reading right now.

See yourself as an author and be willing to ask for (and receive) help and support from your friends and family for the next year as you fully commit to your business. Surround yourself with supportive people. Let them know your intention to create a six-figure (and beyond) business. Let them know how they can help you succeed. It takes a village to build a successful business!

You might want to commit to one year, like I did, to give your business everything you've got. If that seems like too much time, start with a three- or six-month commitment instead. As the author Goethe so eloquently stated: "Until one is committed, there is hesitancy." You cannot create a six-figure business if you're hesitant. A lack of commitment creates the feeling of having your foot on the gas and the brake at the same time, which gets you nowhere.

As I stated above, it's important to openly declare your commitment to creating a successful business to at least one other person. It makes you accountable. You can ask that person to hold you accountable as well. You can ask for support by being clear about what you need. For example, you can ask a friend: "Can you ask me once a week what actions I've taken to grow my business each week?" If you know someone's going to ask you what business actions you've done that week you're much more likely to complete the necessary tasks.

In addition to being accountable, it's also very important to look at the ways in which you may sabotage your success. One of my sabotaging habits used to be returning client calls when I didn't really have time to talk. For example, I'd need to be at a pet sitting job or begin a dog walk in a few minutes, and that's the moment I chose to return a client's call. I would then rush to wrap up the call with the potential client because of my upcoming commitment, and the message that sent to my prospect was, "I don't have time for you."

How did I change that? First, I had to admit I was rushing my client calls in order to fully experience the impact of that behavior: Clients felt rushed and unimportant, and I would sometimes lose a lucrative pet sitting or dog walking opportunity because of the way I handled the initial call. Then I committed to doing things differently: I began giving myself more time in the morning to return client calls. I made certain I set aside large pockets of time in my day to return calls, and eventually I hired a manager to help me manage the phone during those times when I knew I would be especially busy.

I encourage you to look at the ways in which you may be sabotaging your success. If you have a behavior that is limiting your success, no amount of work on everything else I'll cover in this book will help you. Pay attention to those little... and big... sabotaging behaviors that come up this week – the ones that stand in the way of your success. Here are a few that I've helped my coaching clients uncover:

- Spending too much time on Facebook.

- Being snappy or short-tempered with potential new clients.

- Failing to return client calls within 12-24 hours.

- Not keeping track of business expenses.

- Offering clients a discount...even before they've asked for one.

You must be honest with yourself to admit your sabotaging behaviors in order to change them. What are they?

List the sabotaging behaviors that are keeping YOU from experiencing success. Anything you do that makes you cringe goes on the list.

1.

2.

3.

4.

5.

There may also be challenges that stand in your way. I certainly had mine. If you are anything like me, I bet there are areas in your pet sitting business that are going to be challenging as you make this year-long commitment (or however long your commitment to creating business success is).

Here's a sample list of business challenges that one pet sitter gave to me:

1. Billing – It's hard to get those bills out to clients month after month.

2. Dog walking – I really don't like to do it, but it is where a lot of the dependable money is.

3. Returning clients calls – I feel too tired by the end of the day to make them, and during the day I feel too frazzled to do it.

4. Driving like a crazy woman and talking on my cell phone while driving.

List the challenges YOU are experiencing in your business below:

1.

2.

3.

4.

5.

Look over your list, begin to change the way you do the certain items that you wrote down, and don't let those challenges stop you from living your dream of creating a lucrative pet sitting business!

Action Step

Are you willing to work hard for one year in order to create a six-figure pet sitting business? If so, verbally declare it now to your spouse, partner, or friend.

Action Step

If you haven't already done so, complete the list of sabotaging behaviors that are preventing you from experiencing success in your business.

Action Step

Complete the list of the challenges that could potentially keep you from earning six-figures this year if you haven't done so above. Add this Success Statement above your list: "I'm committed to overcoming these challenges in order to create a six-figure pet sitting business by _____." (Enter the date one year from today.) Post the Success Statement and your challenge list where you can see it each day.

Action Step

Get a pen, your journal and a timer. Read the paragraphs below:

Imagine yourself working hard for the next year by taking the actions described in this book. At the end of the year, you are absolutely making more money and feeling more peace as a result of creating a profitable business that works for you. Imagine it is now the date you wrote in the prior action step.

Set the timer for fifteen minutes and write in your journal about what is going on in your life on that date:

Where are you living? How many days a week are you working in your pet sitting business? What are the tasks you are doing in your business? How many staff members do you have? What is the gross (total revenue) and net (income after business expenses) totals that you have made by the end of a solid year's time? Allow yourself to expand beyond any self-imposed beliefs of how your life has been up until now. Allow yourself to really visualize what is possible if you take these proven steps to create the business of your dreams.

Next, place the page(s) in a sealed envelope.

Make a note on the sealed envelope to contact me when you open it a year from now at: success@SixFigurePetSittingAcademy.com to let me know how you did in a year's time. I'd like to hear about your progress!

Finally, put the envelope in your file cabinet or some other place where it will be safe for a year. Be sure to make a note to yourself on your calendar to review it on the date that you wrote above, so you can see how far you have come. I look forward to hearing about your journey!

FIVE

For the Love of Money:

Removing the Blocks
to Let Financial Abundance In

"Money isn't the most important thing in life,
but it's reasonably close to oxygen on the
'gotta have it' scale."

−Zig Ziglar

We've reviewed the business basics, both as an introduction for those starting out and as a review for those who have already launched their pet sitting businesses. You've written a short business plan in less than an hour. And you've defined what success looks like for you and made the commitment to dedicating yourself to doing what it takes to turn your business into a six-figure pet sitting business.

The next step is an important one, and it has nothing to do with spreadsheets, marketing or management of your staff. We'll get to those things, but first, it's important to really understand your relationship with money and to remove the roadblocks that may exist. I wrote earlier that I used some non-traditional methods to achieving my six-figure pet sitting business, and the exercises that follow are some of those non-traditional methods.

Some of you may balk and be unable to see the correlation between the questions I ask in this chapter and how they relate to business. You may wonder how answering them will impact your bottom-line profit margin. You don't really have to know how it relates to your business or your earning potential. You just have to do the exercises and then watch to see what happens in your business and your life as a result of answering the questions.

YOU MUST FIRST UNDERSTAND YOUR REAL RELATIONSHIP WITH MONEY IN ORDER TO TRULY ACHIEVE FINANCIAL SUCCESS.

You'll have to trust me. I've worked with hundreds of coaching clients from around the United States and Canada, and I've seen pet sitters go from making a meager living, living client check to client check, but once they uncovered the blocks to their success... wham! They became six-figure pet sitters. Of course, they are doing all of what is mentioned in this book, in addition to answering the questions that follow. These questions created an awareness, and it was the awareness that created the change. When they consciously became aware of their self-imposed blocks to success and financial abundance, I really saw things begin to shift for them.

So now it's your turn to explore what may hold you back from creating a financially successful pet sitting company.

Set aside 90 minutes of *undisturbed* time to do these exercises that follow. If you don't have 90 minutes now, put down the book and schedule time to do these exercises. Write that 90-minute appointment with yourself for this exercise in your scheduler now. I strongly encourage you to complete this exercise before continuing to read the remaining chapters. You'll reap the most benefit by taking this step before moving on.

If you're ready to focus for 90 minutes, let's get started.

Personal Road Map

The answers to these questions will be your personal map. Your answers, along with the rest of this book, are crucial for your success and will guide you on your journey to creating a six-figure pet sitting business.

Please note: some of these questions are only for pet sitters who have already started their pet sitting businesses. If you haven't yet started your business, then simply answer the ones that apply to you and your current position in your start-up process.

Starting out

Pick a quiet, comfortable place away from distraction.

Tools you'll need

- A timer
- Your journal
- A pen or pencil
- The willingness to discover some new things about yourself and your new or existing business.

Set the timer for 90 minutes and close your eyes. Sit quietly for a moment while imagining the answer to this question:

What could earning six-figures provide that I don't currently have in my life at this moment?

List all the items or qualities of life that earning six-figures might provide:

1. _____

2. _____

3. _____

4. _____

5. _____

6. _____

7. _____

8. _____

9. _____

10. _____

Note: If you are stuck, here are some examples:

- Financial freedom

- Adventure/travel

- Resources to care for my family

- Nice country home

- A horse of my own

- Retirement

- 3-day work week

Notice one of the answers is not simply "more money." To want money just for money's sake will not inspire you to actually create a six-figure business. But knowing WHY you want it…that will get you closer to achieving it.

So now you know what you want for yourself and your life when you create more money in your pet sitting business. Let's explore what may keep you from creating a six-figure income.

Uncovering the Negative Beliefs that Hold You Back

Everyone has negative beliefs about something. Some people can earn money effortlessly, which means their negative beliefs lie elsewhere.

I'm no exception. I had to work through my negative beliefs about money in order to create the financial success I have today. Like most pet sitters, I worked at consistent marketing and other revenue-producing actions to increase my prosperity. Though my financial state improved somewhat because of the actions I took, I did not begin to consistently create the kind of financial success

I now enjoy until I uncovered my negative beliefs about money. Uncovering negative beliefs is like clearing the ground before setting the foundation upon which a pet sitting business can thrive. This is why it's so important for you to take this step and work through these exercises now. Even the strongest structure will not last on a shaky foundation. Your business is no different.

You may think you don't have any negative beliefs regarding money because you know you *want* to earn money. *Wanting* money and actually being able to *create* financial prosperity on a consistent basis, however, are two distinctly different things.

By doing the exercises I've included in this chapter, I was able to clearly see my hidden beliefs about money and bring them to the surface. Only after they were uncovered was I able to work through them. My inner negative beliefs regarding money created an outer lack of money. My outer life was reflecting what was going on internally and mentally regarding certain beliefs that I had about money and about life.

THE BELIEFS WE HAVE ON THE INSIDE MANIFEST ON THE OUTSIDE.

It didn't happen overnight, but over time and once I consciously worked through my negative beliefs, the floodgates to money opened! By doing the inner work combined with the nuts and bolts of running a successful business, I was easily and effortlessly able to create a financially prosperous business.

I know the same can happen for you. You can start your own inner process now by exploring your negative beliefs around money.

Conscious Beliefs about Money:

Sit quietly for a few minutes and think about the money adages that you've heard through the years and what you've heard your parents say about the subject of money.

One I heard often growing up was: "Money doesn't grow on trees."

Write down terms you heard often growing up and/or adages you often have heard about money:

1. _____

2. _____

3. _____

4. _____

5. _____

Uncovering Unconscious Beliefs about Money:

For me to uncover my unconscious beliefs about money, I had to look at where I first learned about money – from my parents and their own relationship with money. Though my parents did well financially, I often witnessed stress about money and paying bills. My dad always seemed to be working hard in order to make more money. He was often exhausted, and the only time I'd see him be still was when he was napping!

Looking at my parents' beliefs about money helped me uncover the hidden beliefs I'd picked up by observing them because I could see them so clearly reflected in my own life before I started this inner process. When I explored my parents' beliefs and how they related to my own money-making abilities, I realized that the predominant belief I had about money and work was:

Making money has to be hard. Work is hard. To make enough money, I have to work hard and be exhausted and wake up and do it again the next day.

What were/are some of your parents' beliefs about money?

Write those parental beliefs about money here:

1. _____

2. _____

3. _____

4.   _____

5.   _____

How do the parental beliefs you witnessed while growing up manifest in your own life today? An example would be: My 'money only comes from working hard' belief showed up in my life through working 7 days a week and often 12 to 14 hours a day.

Write how your parent's beliefs affect your life/business/money today:

1.   _____

2.   _____

3.   _____

4.   _____

5.   _____

Noticing the Contradictions to Money Beliefs

Once I identified my conscious and unconscious beliefs around money, I could then begin to contradict them. This allowed me to begin facing in the direction of financial prosperity. I began to notice the people in my life who I admired because they defied the financial beliefs that I had carried with me for much of my life.

Sometimes I had to wade through the discomfort of jealousy of what that person had in life that I did not yet have. Experiencing the jealousy toward the people in my life who had what I wanted was an unexpected and very uncomfortable part of this process for me! Yet through my willingness to experience the discomfort of jealousy and observe these people who defied my limiting financial beliefs, I was eventually able to see that many of my negative beliefs about money were a lie.

If they had what I wanted, then I could also create that for myself. But it required me to put down my old belief and pick up a different one – a belief that supported my vision of financial prosperity.

List the people currently in your life or those you have observed in the past who seem have what you want regarding financial prosperity. If you admire or feel jealous of someone's financial state, it's definitely a sign that they should go on your list! One of my examples is my friend Tamara's husband: He works 10 hours a week and makes six-figures. List the names along with what that particular person seems to have that you also want:

1. _____

2. _____

3. _____

4. _____

5. _____

Twinges of Awareness

How much do you want to make this year in your pet sitting business? State your desired amount <u>out loud</u> and in the <u>present</u> tense now:

"I make $_____ this year in my pet sitting business."

Sit quietly for five minutes. Listen to the negative responses you hear in your head as a result of having just said that statement out loud.

After 5 minutes have passed, write your negative mental responses to the above statement here:

1. _____

2. _____

3. _____

4. _____

5 _____

Now write positive statements in present tense that contradict each negative mental statement above:

1. _____

2. _____

3. _____

4. _____

5. _____

One negative response I had when I did this exercise was "It will take a lot of hard work for me to make $100,000 a year." (Remember my limiting belief about how making money had to be hard?) My positive statement turned into: "Making $100,000 a year is easy and effortless." If I had contradictory thoughts that arose with my positive statement, I would review my list of people who have what I wanted. They were the role models who dispelled my beliefs about money. If they could do it, so could I. And so can you.

Now write the names of the people on your list who have what you want next to the positive statements above. It will remind you that they have actually achieved what you want to create. It is possible!

Letting the Money In

As I started looking deeply into my own awareness regarding money and what inner beliefs were holding me back from earning six-figures, I also began to notice something else which surprised me. It was a twinge of wanting to push large amounts of money away! It was so subtle at first that I almost didn't notice it.

Here's what the twinge of pushing money away would look like: Let's say I received a large check from a pet sitting client who was going away for two weeks. I would receive the check in the mail, open it up quickly and put it away just as quickly without really allowing myself to enjoy the experience of having just received this large check. The experience of pushing away money was so subtle that when I did become aware of it, I would rationalize it by saying something like this to myself, "I'm not pushing money away. I'm in a hurry and need to put the check away so I can move on to my client calls."

When I allowed myself to simply hold the large check or sit for a moment and look at the large credit card amount I'd just processed, I felt uncomfortable! Until I went through this exercise, I had no idea that it was uncomfortable for me to be in the presence of large sums of money. That discomfort about having large amounts of money coming in was not going to help my desire of *making* large amounts of money, now was it?

> **I WANTED TO EARN MORE MONEY, SO I WAS SHOCKED TO LEARN I HAD AN INGRAINED HABIT OF PUSHING IT AWAY.**

Here I was saying I wanted money, but when it showed up, I began to notice I wanted to push it away. If I hadn't been so attentive in working through my beliefs regarding money, I probably wouldn't even have noticed the subtle pushing away of money. And despite all my work and efforts on effectively running my business, without this realization, I do not believe I would have achieved the financial success I now enjoy.

In order to rectify this problem, the next time I received a large amount of money, I sat with the check and wrote about it:

"This was too easy. I just received $2,000, of which $1,000 is profit for me for my client's long trip. I made $1,000 in a 5-minute phone call of setting up my client with one of my pet sitters. I can't believe that I just made $1,000 in a 5-minute phone call. It's unbelievable! Can making money really be this easy? Now that I have this money, I'm afraid that my client will cancel. I'm afraid that I won't really make this money, but that they will decide not to use my pet sitting service after all. Or if that doesn't

happen, I'm afraid something will go wrong at the sit, and I will have to give this money back to them."

Exercise

Get your journal.

If you have a large pet sitting check or receipt from a credit card transaction that you recently processed, get it and place it in front of you. If you don't have either of those, write a check out to yourself for what you consider to be a large sum and imagine it's from a client. Look at the check and really allow yourself to take in this large amount of money that is now yours. For a few minutes allow yourself to write about your thoughts and feelings regarding this large amount of money.

Deserving money

In addition to uncovering my hidden beliefs about money, I found that my net worth has often also been a reflection of my self-worth.

I could do all the marketing and employ all the business tools I write about in this book, but if my inner value does not match the financial value I want to create, then making large amounts of money just won't happen, no matter how much other work I do. The same is true for you.

List all the reasons why you DO deserve large amounts of money. If you can't think of any reasons make some reasons up. You may find that the made-up reasons are true.

I deserve a lot of money because...

1. _____

2. _____

3. _____

4. _____

5. _____

6. _____

7. _____

8. _____

9. _____

10. _____

Some of your reasons might be:

- I'm 100% committed to providing great care for my clients and their pets.

- I give to charity with what little money I have and if I made more, I'd give more.

- I love what I do and that comes through in my work with animals and clients.

Do You Lack Inner Value?

A symptom of a lack of inner value is often under-earning. This lack of inner value can be made to look productive through marketing and activities to increase your business, but often there is little or no follow through to 'close the deal.' Remember the sabotaging techniques you previously wrote about? A lack of inner value can also sabotage all of your efforts and often will feel as though you, once again, have your foot on the gas and the brake at the same time.

Having a lack of inner value that sabotages your business and financial success is often expressed through:

- Not raising client rates for two or more years.

- Being afraid to say no to a client request.

- Working too hard and not having a lot to show for it.

- Not holding clients to terms outlined in the contract.
- Not having clients sign a contract.
- Giving discounts without clients asking for them.
- Not keeping orderly and accurate business records.
- Being afraid to hire people and/or saying no to new business.
- Returning client calls too late: 24-48 hours later.
- Marketing a lot but feeling too tired to call new clients back.
- Not spending enough time doing revenue-producing activities.

List all the ways you notice that YOU lack inner value and sabotage your business and profit:

1. _____

2. _____

3. _____

4. _____

5. _____

6. _____

7. _____

8. _____

9. _____

10. _____

Now list positive actions you can take to *stop* sabotaging your business and profit (these are often the opposite of what you are currently doing to sabotage):

1. _____

2. _____

3. _____

4. _____

5. _____

6. _____

7. _____

8. _____

9. _____

10. _____

At the beginning of this chapter, I had you write why you deserve a lot of money. Re-list the reasons you noted earlier in this chapter why you deserve large amounts of money. There's a good chance that you will have thought of more since you made that initial list. For example: 'I deserve a lot of money because I am a reliable pet sitter."

I deserve to earn a lot of money in my pet sitting business because...

1. _____

2. _____

3. _____

4. _____

5. _____

6. _____

7. _____

8. _____

9. _____

10. _____

Action Step

Pick one person from your list who you admire and/or whose success you feel jealous about and ask her* if you can discuss beliefs about money with her. Ask her if she has always had the kind of success that she currently has and if not, what does she feel helped her achieve her success. If it feels right, ask her to be a 'money mentor' for you. Let her know you'd like to check in with her every couple of weeks or so as you begin to dismantle your beliefs about money and discuss concerns and questions that arise as you do.

Action Step

Post your positive, present-tense statements that contradict your negative beliefs about money where you can see them every day. Recite them aloud to yourself at least once a day. If you have found a money mentor, ask that person if you can read your positive statements to her.

Action Step

Post your positive actions to combat sabotage where you can see them every day. Commit to taking one concrete positive action each week to counteract a previous sabotaging one and notice the positive effect this action has on your business.

Action Step

Commit to paying attention to money as it comes in, whether you pick up a check from a client's house or whether you receive the checks in the mail. Allow yourself a minute to enjoy the experience of money coming in. Notice if there is any resistance.

**To avoid the awkwardness of writing "her" or "him" constantly, I have sometimes used the feminine pronoun and sometimes the masculine.*

SIX

Rise and Shine:

Creating a Morning Routine
for Business Success

"Always leave enough time in your life to do something that makes you happy, satisfied, even joyous. That has more of an effect on economic well-being than any other single factor."

–Paul Hawkin

Now that you understand the importance of your relationship with money, and have taken some rather unconventional steps and completed exercises that I suspect you thought were unusual at the start, I'd like to introduce you to some other very non-traditional ways to manage your business and run your daily operation.

There are thousands of books written on time management skills and ways to improve efficiency. What I'm about to teach you is a method I have been using for years, and I truly believe it has contributed to my success and helped me create a six-figure pet sitting business. Unlike time-management and organizational tips, this exercise helps unlock your creativity. And I'm sure you'll discover, as I did, that creativity is often the spark you need to achieve business success.

Years ago, I discovered an unusual business tool from an unlikely book. I say "unlikely" because the book was written for artists, not business owners. The book, written by Julia Cameron, is titled *The*

Artist's Way. The tool from *The Artist's Way* that I've found to be incredibly helpful for my business is called 'Morning Pages.'

Morning Pages are simple: You write three pages of whatever you feel like writing. You don't edit. You don't spell-check as you go or after you are finished writing. You let yourself write as sloppily as you want. You basically allow yourself to be imperfect and to write whatever comes to mind. In… the… moment.

You can write about:

- feelings you are having about your teenager.
- the dog that pulls you when you walk him.
- the embarrassed look your neighbor gave you when he slipped.
- your high phone bill.
- the pet sitting client who won't stop complaining.

Anything goes!

The purpose of this, according to author Julia Cameron (and I've found this to be true myself) is that writing three pages of whatever is in your head in the morning gets it out of your head, so that you can focus on the rest of your day. The concept is incredibly simple… and incredibly effective. (I appreciate that some readers, especially those who are just starting their businesses, may already have a very early start to their days. Some coaching clients have questioned if they have to write in the morning. I'm including this activity because I found it so valuable when I was building my six-figure business. You can certainly experiment with writing at other times during the day, but I can attest that writing first thing in the morning has worked wonders for me.)

> **MORNING PAGES HAVE NEVER FAILED TO HELP ME UNLOCK CREATIVE IDEAS THAT HAVE BEEN THE SPARK FOR MANY BUSINESS SUCCESSES.**

I've been writing Morning Pages *every day* since 1990. I've got a shed full of journals to prove it! The biggest gift that I've found is that I may write about whatever is bugging me or fascinating me for the first page or two, but by the time I get to page three, I often get a really great business idea... or realize I need to talk to someone, which will then lead to a particular business venture. It definitely unlocks my creativity, and out of that creativity comes the ideas that I've leveraged for success. Trust me; I would not have continued this exercise unless it was extraordinarily valuable. And it is.

Sometimes when I write, I find that my focus really needs to go in a totally different direction that day, one in which I wasn't planning to go when I first woke up. I may find that taking my day in this different direction results in having a day that flows with ease, joy and financial success as a result of my running my day differently than I'd planned before my Morning Pages.

These are just some of the examples that I've had as a result of my Morning Pages. By doing this exercise, you will have your own story to tell down the road. I find it also helps relieve stress because if I'm struggling with a work or life issue, I can take it to my Morning Pages and really hash it out and get a lot of clarity through the journal writing. A lot of people who write Morning Pages have found them to be the best but most inexpensive therapist, myself included!

Here's what my Morning Page routine looks like:

- Wake up.
- Make tea.
- Light the candle on my dresser.
- Get back into bed with my tea and journal.
- Put tea on nightstand.
- Begin to write.
- Finish after 3 to 5 pages.
- Transcribe any 'to do' ideas I had while writing onto a sticky note to remind myself to do them that day or that week.
- Begin my workday from a clear and focused place.

Your Morning Pages routine may look completely different. That's okay. The important thing is to simply do Morning Pages. At least three pages. Every day.

I've given this action step to coaching clients who are appalled that I, their *business* coach, am recommending that they write in their journal! You may be appalled too. In fact, you may even want to throw this book across the room after having just read about the Morning Pages exercise.

Before you do that, it's important for me to note that the appalled clients of mine have always… *always*… come back to say how much more peaceful, focused, and satisfied they feel in their business and their life after they've spent a couple of weeks writing Morning Pages. They tell me how profitable their business ideas have been as a result of the stream-of-consciousness writing. And how they've discovered things about themselves and the way they've run their businesses they didn't know existed until they started writing.

And the thing is: If you are setting out to make more money in your business than you have ever made in your life, doing something completely different may be exactly what is required to make that happen! If what you've been doing hasn't been working, or if you're struggling to keep your business afloat while maintaining your sanity, what harm is there in trying? That's the message I've shared with my coaching clients, and Morning Pages have worked for them. It can work for you too.

As I shared in my story at the start of this book, I spent a year of doing traditional and non-traditional methods of creating the most profitable pet sitting business that I could. My Morning Pages are, admittedly, one of the non-traditional methods I used. If you do it every morning for a year, you will see results in your business and your life that you could never have imagined. I guarantee it.

Doing this may require some negotiation with your partner regarding childcare, or you may have to wake up a little bit earlier in order to have a quiet morning space in which to write. I encourage you to be willing to do *whatever it takes* to create the success you want in your business and your life. Taking this action will probably result in creating a business and a life that is beyond what you can imagine now. One in which you will look back a year from now and see a lifestyle that will be completely unlike this one you have today!

Develop a Morning Exercise Routine

The second morning routine that I recommend is finding an exercise routine that will enable you to really zone out and let your mind wander. For me, this is an hour-long hike each day.

Because I no longer do dog walking or pet sitting but rather spend my time managing my company, a long hike makes sense for me. If you are walking dogs many hours a day, then obviously a long hike is not going to make sense for you. But let me tell you what I experience during my daily hour-long hike, so that you can discover what your own morning exercise routine might be.

CHOOSE AN EXERCISE ROUTINE THAT LETS YOUR MIND WANDER AND YOU'LL GAIN TWO BENEFITS: GREAT IDEAS AND GOOD HEALTH.

In 2005, I realized that since I was no longer walking dogs, I needed to develop an exercise program, so I could continue to eat whatever I wanted without feeling guilty or having to get new clothes. What I didn't realize was the positive effect exercise would have on my ability to run the business. Here's what happened: I found a hiking trail near my home and began to walk it every morning. I would wake up around 7 a.m., do my Morning Pages, and then return client calls or conduct my coaching sessions. At about 10:00 a.m., I would head out for my morning hike.

What I found on the hike was, after a while, my brain began to really let go, and I began to get some great ideas. Through letting my mind wander on my hike, I might decide to implement a marketing strategy or I might realize I need to have a conversation with a staff member in order to have a better working relationship. There was something about the combination of the Morning Pages and then the hike an hour or two later that really kicked my brain into a creative mode that would enable me to be focused and intentional in my work for the rest of the day.

This didn't happen right away. It happened after a couple of months of hiking the same trail over and over. Why the same trail? I didn't have to think about where to go. I knew the trail like the back of my hand which caused my brain to loosen up in order to get great business ideas and direction for that day's tasks.

You may find that going to the gym has the same effect. Or swimming laps. Or doing yoga. Or Tai Chi. Whatever movement you can do where you can let your mind go is the exercise for you to pick as your morning exercise. Choose something you enjoy and can do without concentrating on it. And remember, it may take several weeks before you find your creative juices flowing as a result of your morning exercise. That's okay. Keep at it because there's a dual benefit. You're getting exercise, and the exercise opens your mind to good ideas and better clarity about your business.

Action Step

Begin tomorrow morning by writing Morning Pages. You can buy a nice journal for this exercise; however, if that is going to cause you to wait to begin your Morning Page practice, a simple notebook or piece of paper will work just fine. Don't delay starting this exercise because you don't have a special journal for your Morning Pages. Whatever you can do to start the process immediately is all that's needed.

Be willing to ask for help if you need assistance with childcare in the morning or set your alarm for 30 minutes earlier than usual and use that time to write.

Commit to doing Morning Pages for a month. If you find that you don't feel more centered, focused and peaceful as a result of doing Morning Pages for 30 consecutive days, then by all means, stop doing them. But I think if you are like most of the pet sitters that I've coached who have used this process, you will probably find that Morning Pages are highly-beneficial in business and in your life. And soon you may find that you can't imagine starting a workday without it!

Action Step

Choose a 45- to 60-minute movement exercise that you can do in the morning by yourself. Remember this is a time for reflection, not work or socialization. If you have to drive to do your movement exercise (hiking trail, gym or other destination), make sure it is not more than a 15-minute drive each way.

Allow your brain to think about everything or nothing, whichever you are in the mood for that day. Even if you find you have 'busy brain', once you are moving for 15 to 20 minutes, your brain should begin to calm down. It's important to do your movement exercise for at least 45 minutes or preferably an hour. It often takes that long for our brains to be quiet and for the creative ideas that must bypass our analytical brain to come through. These are often the best ideas and insights for your business and for the other areas of your life.

Bring a small 'idea book' with you wherever you are doing your morning exercise (pool excluded for obvious reasons) to make note of the ideas and insights that you develop. Ideas are sometimes like dreams – we think we will remember, but a few minutes or hours later the thought is gone.

Commit to doing your morning movement routine for at least 30 days and preferably the same 30 days during which you are trying out the Morning Pages. You will find the combination to be an incredible and empowering start to your day.

Special note: *Leave before 11a.m. to do your morning movement routine. Any later and it will not be morning for long! Plus, you will probably find it may be harder to leave the house or office any later than that. Studies done on exercise routines have found first thing in the morning is the time of day that best sustains a regular, consistent exercise program. Find what works for you and do it.*

Action Step

During the first few weeks of implementing your new writing/exercise routine, take note of the changes that you see begin to happen in your business and your life. I've witnessed dramatic results from coaching clients who participate in this process, and I'd be delighted to hear yours.

SEVEN

Getting Organized:

Daily/Weekly/Monthly Business Organization for Optimum Focus

"One of the secrets of getting more done is to make a TO-DO List every day, keep it visible, and use it as a guide to action as you go through the day."

–Jean de La Fontaine, French poet born 1621

Once your creative juices begin flowing, and I know they will, as a result of establishing your morning routine, you'll need to organize and track all of those ideas. As a business owner, you have a lot of plates in the air at any one time. If you haven't started your business yet, you will too as you prepare to launch your business. Organization is the key to keeping your sanity and converting your pet sitting business into a six-figure one. Some people are born organizers, and some groan at the very thought of it.

Maybe you groaned when you turned the page and read this chapter's title. If that's you – and you're struggling with your business, working long hours without having much, if anything, to show for it at the end of every month – you can keep on doing what you're doing… but don't expect to attain the success I've been talking about. You must be organized in order to be successful, and getting – and staying – organized is not really that difficult.

As with any task or goal, making it manageable makes it work. You can easily regain control of your schedule and get organized by breaking things down into daily, weekly, and monthly activities. But before you grab your planner and start making lists, there's a better place to begin.

Office Cleaning

I've heard it said that the state of our homes, whether organized or messy, is often a reflection of the organized or messy state of our brains. The same idea goes for our offices. If your office is a mess, I recommend you put 'cleaning your office" as the very first task on your to-do list. It's very unlikely that a messy brain can run a six-figure business. Granted, there are exceptions, but they are just those – exceptions.

> **THE STATE OF YOUR HOME, WHETHER MESSY OR ORGANIZED, IS OFTEN A REFLECTION OF THE ORGANIZED OR MESSY STATE OF YOUR BRAIN.**

Working in a messy office is not conducive to creating a six-figure business. Think about any top executives' offices that you've been in (if you haven't been in any top executive offices, think about executives' offices that you've seen in movies). Executives' desks are usually spotless and have a lot of open space on them. This gives them the ability to focus on the task at hand. What's good for a high-powered executive is good for you! Even if you don't strive to be a high-powered executive, I'm betting that you are striving to create a six-figure pet sitting business. In fact, I'm certain of it because you are still reading.

Besides eliminating chaos and creating an environment which enables you to really concentrate on the task at hand, an orderly office is an efficient one. How much time do you waste in any given day looking for paperwork, files or even the stapler, for that matter? Every minute you waste because of clutter is a minute you lose doing a more productive, revenue-generating task. Or every minute you waste is another minute you could be out of the office, enjoying your free time. Clean your office and get organized!

And while you're cleaning and re-organizing, think about where you locate things. Be certain the files, books and supplies you use constantly are close at hand. At the same time, don't waste valuable real estate on your desk by cluttering it with items you don't use very often. The exact same thing is true of your computer desk top. Are icons neat and orderly, making it easy for you to find the document you want or launch the program you need? Or are there icons everywhere, haphazardly causing you to waste time searching before you click?

Getting It Done!

Did you notice the quote at the beginning of this chapter? If not, go back and read it now.

It seems to-do lists have been around for a long time! It doesn't matter if you type or write your to-do lists; what's important is having them and putting them where you can see them each day, so you'll stay on track. I encourage you to break your to-do list down by monthly, weekly and daily tasks.

Monthly Prep: 29th to 31st of each month

Prepare a written list of your next month's goals and important to-do's sometime between the 29th and 31st of each month. You can start with whatever has been grabbing for your attention or those things you have been avoiding.

Any to-do list I write, including my monthly list, has 10 items or fewer on it. I found that having more than 10 items on a list causes me to get stressed. And the point of these lists is to remove stress, not to cause it! An overloaded to-do list becomes overwhelming and creates frustration and failure. This is a case in which less really is more. Writing my list on a standard size sticky note is the perfect way to keep my to-do list to fewer than 10 items. There simply isn't room to write more than ten items.

Include anything on your monthly list that you absolutely must get done this month. Make sure to add the date by which you need to complete each item to keep you on track. Once you've finished writing your list, organize it according to the date by which you need to do each item. Add a star at the end of any item that you might have resistance to doing.

Here is an example of one of my monthly lists:

- Mail in tax payment by January 10.
- Talk to Jenny about managing on Mondays by January 11.
- Update home page text on website by January 14.*
- Renew business insurance by January 14.
- Prepare for taxes by January 20.*
- Create at least 5 new blog posts this month by January 25.
- Get client newsletter out by the January 25.
- Drop off business cards at 15 locations by January 30.*

Treat yourself to something special when you complete any task with a star.

Sunday Prep: Weekly List

Like most business owners, I start my workweek on Monday morning. I use some time on Sunday night to prep for the week by writing out a list of both the next day's to-do's as well as the weekly to-do's. This helps me transition from the weekend to the coming workweek, and it helps me have absolute clarity about what I need to do that week. I've found my Sunday night prep to be one of the most important organizing aspects for my business for the coming week.

Have your weekly list contain:

- Billing/Accounting Tasks
- Marketing ideas
- Hiring steps that need to be taken
- Calls you need to make
- Anything that is tugging at you to do
- What you've avoiding doing but you know you need to do
- Anything from the past week's lists that you haven't done

I may add to the list as the week progresses and as I've crossed off what's already done (remember I don't put any more than 10 items on a list at any one time). Having clarity before I start my workweek helps me hit the ground running as soon as Monday morning begins.

You'll find your weekly list is the idea starter for your daily list as well.

Daily To-Do Lists

Your daily to-do list should start the night before. When I end each workday, I write a clear list of to-do items for the following day. This way, I can really let work go at the end of the day and live my life that night because I know my to-do list is written out and will be waiting for me the next day. I can hit the ground running after spending a pleasant night doing anything but worrying about what's on my schedule for the next day. I've already worked out the details while they were fresh in my mind. Do a quick review of your weekly and monthly lists and include any required tasks from those onto your daily list.

Because I have tea every morning, I write my next day's list on a sticky note and place it on my tea box the night before, so I can see it first thing in the morning. Having my list in a place that I see when I first wake up also enables me to use my Morning Page time to write about that day's to-do list and any resistances I may have to doing that day's actions in addition to whatever else I want to write about that morning.

If there is something I don't want to forget the next day, I will write it on a sticky note and place it on my tea box as well. Sometimes I have three or four sticky notes on my tea box! It's the perfect landing spot for those items that I want out of my brain for the moment but need to remember the next day.

Where can you put your next day's list so you will see it first thing in the morning?

Cross items off your list as you accomplish them. Every time you cross a task off one of your to-do lists, you've taken another step toward success and creating a six-figure business. Keep your lists posted where you can see them every day. Crossing off tasks when you've completed them will also give you a sense of accomplishment. And don't hesitate to reward yourself for completing a challenging to-do item! How do you motivate the pets you care for? With a treat, right? Why not set up a treat system for yourself. For example, "When I finish the billing for the week, I'm going to…" insert your own reward here, and then enjoy it!

Night-Before Prep: 5-minute Cleaning Frenzy

Inevitably, when I end a busy pet sitting day in the office, there are client contracts strewn about and other papers that need to be filed. Not having my office clean and orderly at the end of each workday leads me to feel stressed and anxious when I start my next day of office work. Feeling stressed and anxious is no way to start the day, and it's no way to run a six-figure pet sitting business.

After you've written your to-do list for the next day, your last office task for the night should be to take five minutes to clean your office. At the end of each workday, I set a timer for five minutes and focus on organizing that day's papers and invoices. It's amazing what can be accomplished in five solid minutes of focused attention to cleaning and organizing. Within five minutes, my office is usually spotless. Between a clean office and a next-day to-do list, I am free to go enjoy that night's activities without work or my messy office pulling at me for my attention.

If you had to take a break from reading this book to thoroughly clean and de-clutter your office, take heart. If you spend five minutes at the end of each day on this office task, you'll never have to go through an organizational overhaul again. You may have to dust once on a while, but it'll be easy since you won't have to work around the clutter.

Creating a Time Plan

Creating a time plan for yourself and your business can be one of the most illuminating actions you can take in your business. Why? Because usually we, as business owners, are so focused on the day-to-day tasks that we don't have a clear picture of where our time is going each week or month.

You can create a time plan in Excel (see sample on the following page).

Be sure to include regular personal and business actions, and highlight the different categories, so you can see how your time is spent regarding revenue-producing activities, time with your family and friends, exercise, eating, etc. Create your own categories and have fun with it.

Start with an actual time plan that shows where your time currently goes:

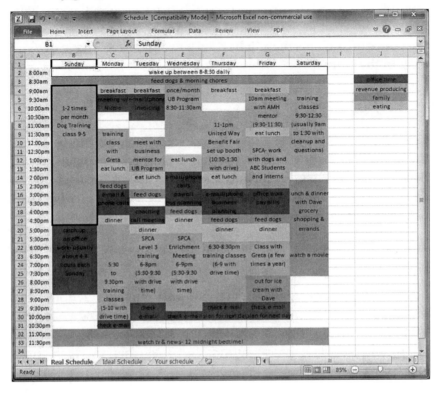

And then create an Ideal Time Plan that shows where you would like your time to go:

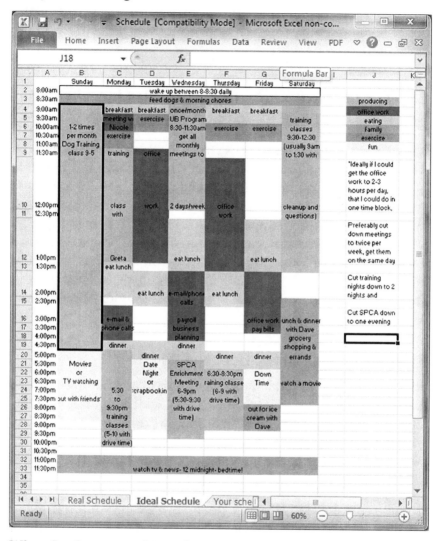

When I ask my coaching clients to create their actual and ideal times plans, most of them fill all of the spaces. It's important to allow some 'blank' space in each day for emergencies that may arise and/or to allow for spontaneity in each day. Be sure to include time blocks that make sense to you in yours.

It's also important to look at where are your revenue-producing activities occur. Some pet sitters who are struggling financially and who use these time plans, realize that they are not putting enough time into revenue-producing activities. So then they begin focusing on incorporating more of the 'green areas' (office and direct revenue-producing activities) into their time and usually their profit margin will rise!

Calling in Your Tribe to Help You Organize & Offer Support

As business owners, we're often used to doing things ourselves. As a self-employed business owner you probably fall into that category as well. We forget that we can ask for help. Help doesn't even have to come in the form of someone doing the work for us. It can simply be someone supporting us in our work. Being supported often nurtures success, at least it has in my case. I'd like to share a few ways that I've found to get invaluable support that helped me immensely on my way to creating my six-figure pet sitting business. I believe you'll find the business support suggestions below equally helpful to build the business of your dreams as well.

Business Support Tool: Bookending

Bookending is a valuable tool which involves phoning a friend before you are about to begin an activity which requires courage, attention or a large portion of time. Simply call your friend and say what it is you are about to do, why the task is challenging and what you are committed to accomplishing. Let him know that you will call him when you complete your task.

If you get voicemail, leave a detailed message. It's not about reaching a live person, it's about being accountable, and sometimes just knowing you've left a message that your friend will hear is enough to help you do that.

Business Support Tool: Daily Check-in with an Action Buddy

Do you know of another business owner who you could support and who could support you? Ask that person if she would be willing to receive your e-mails in the morning or receive a short phone call detailing what you will be doing that day. Let her know you will also e-mail or call at the end of the work day to report on your accomplishments. Tell her that you would like to be there for her in this same way, so that she can be accountable to stay on track with her daily tasks as well.

Here are some ideas to make this a supportive experience for both of you:

- Decide on a regular time that you will e-mail or call. Determine who will call whom if you are using the phone to check in.

- If you do use the phone to check in with your daily action buddy, keep the call short and all business. This is not about talking about personal information unless the two of you agree to that. You can do that after your workday has ended. This is about both of you staying on track with what you are committed to accomplishing that day.

- Agree to not offer advice about the other person's actions unless it is requested. Agree to support each other and cheer each other on, not give unsolicited advice.

- Decide on the length of time for which you will try this action. Two to four weeks is a good time frame in which you can determine if you are the right supportive fit. If it's a good fit, keep it going! You'll both benefit.

Business Support Tool: Bi-weekly Record-keeping Lunch

Business owners are often an isolated group of people. Especially pet sitters! We are on the phone or with animals but rarely face-to-face with people. That is one of the reasons that I have found this support tool so helpful in my own life. It involves regular ongoing contact with a friend.

Here's how it works:

1. Find a friend who is self-employed or has a very flexible work schedule. Widen your support net by picking a friend who is not your daily action buddy!

2. Decide on a regular day to meet at each other's home every other week to do record keeping and/or billing or other business tasks that can be easily done at someone else's home or on your laptop.

3. Decide if you want to make lunch for each other. If so, take turns hosting the meeting and preparing the food.

4. Enjoy chatting about the past two weeks for an hour but then get down to business after the hour lunch has ended.

5. Do your record keeping or whatever else you brought to work on for 90 minutes or so.

Action Step

Daily Prep and 5-minute end-of-the-workday cleaning frenzy: Write your daily to-do list the night before. Determine where you always go in the morning and post your daily list there, so that you to see it first thing in the morning. Put the 5-minute cleaning frenzy on your list until it becomes a regular, end-of-the-day habit. Notice how good you feel when you start your workday with a tidy desk and office.

Action Step

Office organization: If your office needs more than a 5-minute cleaning frenzy then put a 30-minute office cleaning session on your daily to-do list and do as many 30-minute cleanings that are needed until your office is tidy and organized.

Action Step

Weekly and Monthly Prep: Mark on your calendar on Sundays and the 29th of each month to do weekly and monthly prep and commit to doing what you've written down. Print out your weekly and monthly list when you create them and put them where you can see them each day. Enjoy crossing things off the list. Notice how much more focused you become and how much you accomplish.

Action Step

Create an actual time plan and an ideal time plan. Color code the different categories that define the different activities that define where your time goes. Be sure to include blank space in your ideal time plan! Hire an Excel expert to help you if you can't create an Excel time plan on your own.

Action Step

Opt for one or more of the Support Tools listed in this chapter. Notice how your business improves simply by giving and receiving support from another business owner.

EIGHT

Show me the Money!

Understanding and Working with Basic Business Financials

*"Motivation is what gets you started.
Habit is what keeps you going."*

–Jim Ryun

By now you've gotten clear on what you want to create and why. You've made the necessary commitment. You now understand the blocks to letting money flow in, and you are correcting them. You have a morning routine that will create a platform from which to jump off of into your day. You are getting organized in your office and business tasks. You are now ready to move on to clarity around the money itself.

Pet sitters often groan when I ask to see their spreadsheets of revenue and personal/business expenses. I ask them for these items because I realize there is POWER in having clarity about how much is earned and how much is spent. Trust me.

I've run my business both ways: without clarity and with clarity. I can tell you that choosing to have clarity about how much money was coming in and how much money was going out is one of the reasons that I run a highly successful, six-figure pet sitting business today.

Consider this:

- If you don't know how much you earn, you can't set goals.

- If you can't set goals, you will be successful "by accident" and not on purpose.

- If you are not successful on purpose, then you cannot recreate your success year after year after year.

When I ask pet sitters how much they are making each month, they often have no idea. If they *do* know how much they are earning each month they will usually give me their gross total. The gross total that is their total revenue... the total of incoming checks and credit card charges. Yes, this gross amount is the total revenue, but it does not reflect the real earnings as it has not taken business expenses into consideration. Your real earnings are your net profit. And put simply, net profit is your total revenue less your expenses. Whatever is left over when you subtract your total expenses (including all required federal, state and local tax payments) from your total revenue is *your* money.

Your net profit is the number that you want to work to increase each month! There are two simple ways to increase your net profit: Generate more revenue or reduce expenses.

It's been my experience that more money is made as a direct result of taking the time to get clarity about your numbers... to really understand how much is coming in (and from where) and how much is going out (and where it's going). Having clean, orderly accurate numbers in your business creates a container to generate more revenue.

Here are some excuses that coaching clients often give me about why they haven't or don't want to get clarity on their revenue and expenses:

Coaching client: "I don't have time to create a financial spreadsheet."

Kristin: You don't have time not to.

Coaching client: "I can't figure out Excel or Quicken or QuickBooks."

Kristin: Hire someone this week to help you. Put an ad on Craigslist. There are lots of people who love teaching about the financial program of your choice. They can come to your home and help.

Coaching Client: "I have all my expense receipts but I don't know what categories to put my expenses under."

Kristin: It's easy. Here are the categories. (And readers, I'll share those categories with you shortly.)

Very simply, there's no excuse for lacking clarity about your income and expenses. Prosperity and wealth are impossible without a crystal clear vision of your finances.

Let's begin with "Record keeping made easy in 10 steps":

1. Buy a small expense notebook and keep it in your purse or wallet.

2. If it is spiral-bound, put a pen in the spiral. Keep it simple… and handy.

3. Enter everything that you spend your money on. Everything.

4. Use the categories I've provided to categorize your entries.

5. Write down what you spent as soon as you buy something, not a few hours later. You'll forget.

6. Create a spreadsheet of your revenue and separate staff-earned and you-earned (example follows). Enter revenue as it comes in.

7. At the end of each month, highlight your business expenses in your expense notebook and enter your business expenses in the appropriate category in your business expense spreadsheet.

8. All personal categories will not be highlighted. Next enter those in your personal expense spreadsheet.

9. Total all of your revenue/expenses.

10. Deduct your business expenses from your total revenue. This is your <u>net profit</u>.

Below you will find my suggested list for sample expense categories for both business and personal expenses. Add your own or deduct those that aren't applicable to your particular business or situation.

Personal Expenses:

Acupuncture
Auto Expenses
Auto Repair-personal car
Beauty
Bike
Chai/Coffee
Chiropractic
Clothing
Creativity
Credit Card Repayment
Décor-Home
Entertainment
Food-in
Food-out
Gardening
Gifts
Gifts for myself
Vitamins/Health
Health Club Membership

Hot Tub
Household
Laundry (Dry Clean)
Massage
Medical Premium
Therapy
Music
Optical
Savings-Periodics
Savings-Prudent Reserve
Savings-Travel
Sports
Tithe
Toiletries
Travel
Rent/Mortgage
Taxes-Federal
Taxes-State
TOTAL PERSONAL EXPENSES:

Business Expenses:

Accounting
Advertising-online
Advertising-print
Advertising-newsletters
Advertising-Help Wanted
Auto-expenses-work car
Auto-insurance
Auto loan-work car
Bank Charges
Books
Misc. Business Supplies
Cell Phone
Computer
Computer Admin System
Contracted Work
Education
Gas

Insurance-Business
Janitorial
Licenses
Membership
Office Supplies
Pet Supplies
Phone
Restaurant
Toll, Parking
Utilities
Website
TOTAL BUSINESS EXPENSES:
TOTAL REVENUE:
TOTAL NET PROFIT:

SIX-FIGURE SUCCESS TIP

Determine your Net Profit each month by taking your total revenue (income) and deducting all of your business expenses. Often pet sitters (and other business owners) will say, "I make $10,000 a month," when that is GROSS (total) revenue and not the net profit. The net profit is what you ACTUALLY make each month, after your expenses. That is the true figure of what you earn.
What was your net profit last month? Last year?
Get clarity and watch your income grow!

Please note that the categories examples I've included contain only some of the possible personal and business categories that you may have. Be sure to check with your accountant to gain clarity about what expenses you have that you may be able to declare as a business expense.

Excel spreadsheets

Excel is an easy-to-use program that will help you create professional spreadsheets that enable you to get an overall picture of your revenue as well as business and personal expenses at a glance.

Here's a sample personal expense Excel spreadsheet:

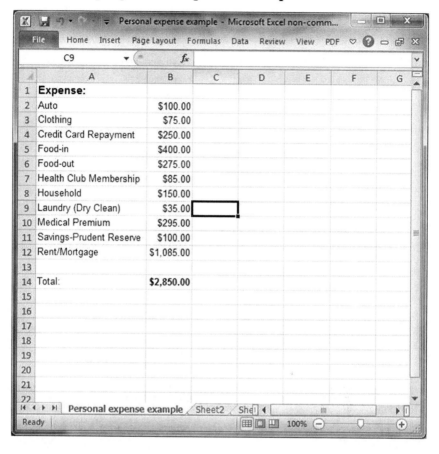

	A	B	C	D	E	F	G
1	**Expense:**						
2	Auto	$100.00					
3	Clothing	$75.00					
4	Credit Card Repayment	$250.00					
5	Food-in	$400.00					
6	Food-out	$275.00					
7	Health Club Membership	$85.00					
8	Household	$150.00					
9	Laundry (Dry Clean)	$35.00					
10	Medical Premium	$295.00					
11	Savings-Prudent Reserve	$100.00					
12	Rent/Mortgage	$1,085.00					
13							
14	Total:	$2,850.00					

Here's a sample business excel spreadsheet:

	A	B	C	D	E	F	G
			fx =C18-C17				
7	Cell Phone		$69.00				
8	Insurance-Business		$87.00				
9	Janitorial		$48.00				
10	Office Supplies		$178.00				
11	Pet Supplies		$432.00				
12	Phone		$89.00				
13	Restaurant		$141.00				
14	Toll, Parking		$68.00				
15	Website		$227.00				
16							
17	Total Expenses:		$2,004.00				
18	Total Revenue:		$8,342.00				
19	Net Profit:		$6,338.00				
20							
21							
22							
23							

Business expense example / Sheet2 / Sheet3

SIX-FIGURE SUCCESS TIP

If you don't know how to use Excel, don't forget to ask an Excel-savvy friend or hire someone to help you. It is not difficult to learn the basics you'll need. Having your numbers in a clear Excel spreadsheet is a powerful business tool. It will give you complete clarity about how profitable your business actually is.

Categories for Revenue Streams

A few years ago, I wanted to stop offering dog walking service to our clients because I found it to be so much work: Clients switching days, dog walkers going on vacation and my lack of back-up dog walkers, etc.

Thank goodness I had decided a few months prior to keep track of my various revenue streams; thus, I was able to easily see how much I was making from the dog walking service. When I looked at my total earned for dog walking, it was as much as all of our other services combined! (50% of my pet sitting business's gross revenue!)

If I had quit the dog walking revenue stream, my business would have experienced a 50% loss of revenue! Instead, I was able to shift my focus to fixing this revenue stream's 'pain points' rather than suspend this revenue-producing segment of my business. To fix those pain points, I began to clearly communicate with clients about our need for set days, and I hired back-up walkers to cover the regular walkers' vacations. Now dog walking is a breeze, *and* I still have all that revenue coming in.

If you are not already doing it, keep track of your revenue each month for your various revenue streams. It's never a wise decision to make business decisions without having all the facts.

Here are the typical revenue streams you track:

- Cat Visits – staff
- Dog Visits – staff
- Dog Walking – staff
- Overnight – staff
- Cat Visits – me
- Dog Visits – me
- Dog Walking – me
- Overnight – me
- Total Staff Revenue Stream
- Total 'Me' Stream

What are your various revenue streams and/or what kinds of revenue streams would you like to create in your business?

1. _____

2. _____

3. _____

4. _____

5. _____

6. _____

7. _____

8. _____

9. _____

10. _____

Monthly and Yearly Revenue Comparisons

You will also want to total your monthly revenue and include it in a yearly spreadsheet (see January and February example below). Without this, you will be unable to determine your revenue averages each month and over the course of the year. This will help you plan accordingly for the slow months and also enable you to see how far you've come in the course of a year after doing the exercises in this book! It will also help you more easily set and keep revenue goals each month.

Here's an example of what a monthly/yearly revenue comparison chart looks like:

REVENUE COMPARISON: 2005 TO 2011

	JANUARY	FEBRUARY
2005	16,002.12	15,992.00
2006	18,677.00	14,269.50
2007	21,430.00	18,145.00
2008	22,792.61	20,680.00
2009	25,436.23	21,490.20
2010	26,422.74	23,401.43
2011	30,526.98	26,491.18

You can imagine how this chart will expand to the right with a column for the remaining months of the year, and how it will expand downward with each year you add. A yearly revenue comparison spreadsheet is very easy to create in a program like Excel. Learn it or pay someone to help you set it up. A quick glance at this chart also indicates a trend for this particular business: February has always produced less revenue than January. In this case, you would plan your February expenses accordingly, knowing that there's going to be less money coming in. In looking at this data, you may also want to consider a special marketing promotion in February to boost revenue!

The Importance of Separating Your Business and Your Personal Bank Accounts

For years, I had one checking account into which I deposited all of my checks. I used the same account to pay for my business and personal expenses. Even though I heard over and over from my business-owning friends about the importance of maintaining separate accounts, I didn't get a personal account because I thought having one account would keep things simple.

When I finally did get a personal checking account to pay all of my personal expenses and only used the business account to pay business expenses, I was surprised to discover a level of freedom and healthy separation from my business that was unexpected. I also found that having separate personal and business checking accounts made it much easier to keep track of business and personal expenses.

Many pet sitters that I coach do exactly what I used to do: They have one bank account into which they deposit their business checks, and they use that business account to pay for their business *and* their personal expenses. By separating your business and personal accounts, you will find that it will bring you one step closer to having a business and also having a life.

Pay yourself a salary

After separating your business and personal accounts, you'll find it much easier to pay yourself a salary. The easiest way to determine how much you can afford to pay yourself is: Add up your personal expenses and then pay yourself half of that amount on the 1st of each month and half on the 15th. Obviously, you are going to have to do some balancing as you begin and grow your business. You may have to cut back on personal expenses to avoid bankrupting your business. But remember, you're on your way to generating a six-figure pet sitting business like I did. When you achieve that success, you will most likely not be worrying about what you can and can't afford.

Savings Accounts

Everyone knows the importance of saving, but not very many people do it. Make a commitment to yourself today to set aside at least five to ten percent of what you are earning each month and put it into your savings account.

I have my savings automatically transferred each month from my business account into my savings account. In this way, it becomes part of my automatic monthly expense – I don't think about it except when I deduct it each month in my check register on the date of the automatic transfer.

I have many savings accounts for both business and personal savings and I encourage you to set up as many savings accounts as you need. Most savings accounts are free if you have at least $300 or more in them.

Here are different savings account categories to set up which will make savings a breeze:

Four Business Savings Accounts:

1. **Business: Periodic Expenses** ~ For yearly expenses like business insurance and membership fees.

   How: Determine this amount by adding up those recurring yearly expenses that you paid out last year and divide it by twelve. Then funnel that monthly amount into your periodics account. Often these yearly expenses can cause us to go into debt because we forget about them until the big bill arrives. If you save, you will be prepared.

2. **Business: Prudent Reserve** ~ Save for at least six months' worth of expenses in case of severe illness or emergency.

   How: Determine this amount by adding up the last year's business and personal expenses and divide that by twelve. Then figure out how much six months of that would be and begin to set aside a minimum amount.

3. **Business: Tax Payments** ~ Ensure you can pay your quarterly and yearly taxes on time.

   How: Set aside 20 to 25 percent of your gross revenue in a tax account, so you pay your quarterly and yearly tax payments in a timely manner. I'll discuss taxes more in depth in the following section.

4. **Business: Gifts** ~ For holiday gifts and bonuses for staff and holiday gifts for clients.

   How: Determine how much/what you want to give your staff and clients over the course of a year. Save a minimum of $25 per month in the special savings account you've allocated for staff/client gifts.

Personal Savings Accounts:

Don't forget about your personal accounts! Here are some examples of personal savings accounts that you may want to set up:

Personal: Periodic Expenses ~ For those sometimes unexpected but recurring personal expenses.

Personal: Prudent Reserve ~ Set aside a minimum of six months' worth of personal expenses. This savings account should only be used in an emergency.

Personal: Gifts ~ Determine how much you want to spend (or do spend) on gifts for friends and family and begin to set aside money now.

Personal: Travel ~ Determine where you want to go, how much it will cost to get you there as well as accommodations and perks and begin setting money aside for your dream trip!

Personal: Clothing ~ Determine how much you want to spend on clothing per year and set aside a portion each month.

Personal/Business: Retirement ~ Talk to your accountant about how much you should set aside and what kind of retirement account is best for you. There are special IRAs for self-employed people and putting money into these accounts will help you save for the future and reduce your tax liability.

Taxes and Quarterly Payments

When I first started my pet sitting business many years ago, I had another job that was my main source of income while I started pet sitting. That job helped me get on my feet until I could rely on my pet sitting business as my main source of income. For the first couple of years, I didn't make a lot in my pet sitting business, so I didn't have to pay a lot (if anything) in taxes.

The year after I began running my business full-time, I was in for a rude awakening! I hadn't paid any estimated federal taxes. On April 15, I owed the government over $8,000 for the prior year's taxes. Ouch.

Since I didn't have any money in savings, I created a payment plan with the IRS which resulted in the original $8,000 tax bill ballooning to over $16,000 over the course of the few years that it took to pay it off. Let me share a little-known fact about the IRS: When you opt for a payment plan through the IRS, you are charged huge amounts of compounded interest and penalties even if you are now paying your late taxes in a timely manner and with a payment plan. The IRS wants the money it's owed, when it's owed. And if they don't get it, you pay!

Having this $16,000 tax debt felt like my business was sinking fast. If my business was a boat, then the IRS tax debt was an ever-growing hole in the hull. Just as quickly as I was scooping water out of the boat, twice as much water was coming in (that's compound interest for you).

Through the process of incurring my tax debt and paying it off, I learned five important tax tips that I'd like to share with you:

1. **Get a good accountant.** Preferably someone who works with small businesses and who will be able to point out all of the intricate deductions and expenses that a small business owner can take. Having a good accountant

will cost you more money at tax time but will save you thousands of tax dollars each year.

How do you find a good accountant? Ask other business owners or friends for a referral. Or look in the phone book and 'interview' accountants over the phone. Don't be afraid to ask for references if you're finding someone out of the phone book. Once you have those references, check them!

I encourage you to find an accountant who is not just a "numbers" person but also a "people person." It's best to find someone you can really converse with about your pet sitting business and who will give you tips for saving money and running a more effective business. Remember: Most accountants deal with small businesses daily. They can often provide a wealth of information about how best to run your business. You want to find someone with whom you can relate and with whom you feel can guide you in maintaining a prosperous and solvent business in addition to completing your tax forms.

When you find the right accountant, set up an appointment as soon as possible! Commit to a date by which you will interview accountants and make a hire. April 1st is when a lot of pet sitters suddenly remember that tax time is coming and that is NOT a good time to start interviewing. Besides, unless you're already a client, few accountants will speak to you between April 1st and the 15th!

2. **If you have not yet set aside anything for taxes, begin today: Put aside as much money as you can in your designated tax savings account, so that you can make a payment to the IRS by April 15th.**

Some pet sitters complain to me that they can't save for taxes because they're not making enough to cover daily expenses. Look, if you had a car repair bill or an emergency dental procedure that needed to happen, you'd find the money, right? Any timely payment to the IRS is better than nothing. Make a firm commitment to yourself that 20 to 25 percent of all income earned from clients between now and

April 15 goes into a tax savings account. No ifs, ands or buts about it. Trust me; I would have much preferred to spend $8000 on anything other than IRS penalties and interest.

Typically, the most common way to pay the IRS is with a quarterly payment. In fact, after your first year in business, the IRS will be looking for that payment every quarter. Determine how much you'll owe in quarterly taxes (or ask your accountant) and be certain you set aside one third of that amount every month. For example, if your tax payments are $3000 for the quarter, add $1000 to your monthly expense spreadsheet and set those funds aside. Once you have a better feel for your tax percentage, you can simply set aside that percentage from every single check or credit card payment you receive.

If you find yourself spending your tax money, then I would encourage you to mail your quarterly tax payment monthly! Remember: It's not really your money, and when you face penalties and interest, you'll even have less of what really is your money. To pay monthly, simply make copies of your quarterly IRS payment coupons and send a third of your quarterly payment each month. Putting an envelope addressed to the IRS with your monthly bills will help you remember to send your payment on time and to budget for it each month.

Depending on your state, you may have to pay state income tax in addition to federal tax. Be sure to check with your accountant about state tax requirements. You can also ask your accountant how much he or she recommends you should set aside of your total revenue in order to pay your taxes in full each year.

3. **Be diligent about keeping track of every payment you receive and record each payment in a computer program like Quicken or Quickbooks.**

I've used both software systems, and Quicken seems to be the easier program to use for first time record-keepers.

As I mentioned earlier, if you need someone to train you on Quickbooks or Quicken, simply put an ad on www. Craigslist.org to find a Quickbooks or Quicken expert to help you. Most pet sitting administration software systems will help you keep track of your revenue, so you won't have to do this step.

4. **Recording daily business expenses every time you make a business purchase or write a check makes tax time much easier!**

Remember my "Recordkeeping made easy in 10 steps" from earlier in this chapter? This is where it really comes in handy. I keep a small notebook in my purse, and *every* amount I spend on the business (staff checks, office supplies, etc.) gets written in this book immediately after I've written the check. At the end of the month, I enter all my expenses in Quicken and tally it up at the end of the year for easy tax preparation. Tax time can be stressful enough; having my expense records already itemized at the end of each calendar year makes taxes a breeze.

5. **If you cannot pay the amount you owe to the IRS, do everything you can to *avoid* a payment plan with the IRS.**

Remember how my tax payment of $8,000 ballooned to a hefty $16,000 in only a few years because I had a payment plan with the IRS? The IRS charges extremely high interest *and* late payment fees. If you are on a payment plan, you are already considered a late payee, so you get penalized twice with high interest!

If you have good credit, you can put the amount on a credit card and move the tax balance to a 0% credit card for 12 to 18 months (depending upon the terms). When I did this years ago, there was a balance-transfer fee (2.5% of the balance I transferred) when I used the 0% credit card that I got for my tax debt, but it was worth it because helped me pay down the $16,000 balance, and I avoided even more interest in the long run!

Does this sound like a big headache? You bet it does. The best way to avoid this stress is to pay your taxes when they're due. No one likes dealing with taxes, but good preparation this year can help you have a relaxed tax experience next year.

While you are talking to your accountant about taxes, ask about retirement accounts so that you can save on your tax bill. As I mentioned earlier, there are special IRAs for self-employed people, and putting money into these accounts will help you save for the future and save on your taxes.

Action Step

Purchase a record-keeping book and carry it with you. Whether business or personal, cash or credit, write down every purchase you make. Refer to the section "Record Keeping in 10 Easy Steps" to begin to keep track of your personal and business expenses.

Action Step

Use Quicken or QuickBooks to create a clear record of your business and personal expenses and as a means of separating them. If you don't know how to use an accounting software system, ask for help.

Action Step

Use Excel to create a spreadsheet like the one on pages 89-90. If you don't know how to use Excel, ask for help.

Action Step

Begin to track your monthly/yearly revenue and gross profit comparison in an Excel spreadsheet. If you have been in business for a year or longer and you have accurate records of your gross profit, then create an Excel spreadsheet that details all the months you've been in business to date. Note the months that are consistently slower pet sitting periods and the months where your profit suddenly shot up. Be a detective and find out why your profit was so high in certain months and not in others. Continue to make monthly entries and review the comparison.

Action Step

Determine what your various revenue streams are and create categories in Quicken or QuickBooks.

Action Step

Determine your average monthly personal expenses and pay yourself a salary. If you don't already have one, get a personal checking account in addition to a business account.

Action Step

Set up savings accounts for periodic expenses and prudent reserve for both business and personal savings. Include other areas of your life/ business that you would like to create savings accounts for.

Action Step

If you don't already have one, get a good accountant. Pay quarterly taxes by the date due. If you owe back taxes to the IRS, payoff the total with savings or a 0% or low-interest rate credit card. In this way, you will stop your business boat from leaking!

NINE

You Are What Your Clients See:

Creating Great Promotional Materials

"A brand that captures your mind gains behavior.
A brand that captures your heart gains commitment."

–Scott Talgo, Brand Strategist

You've heard that you never get a second chance to make a good first impression, right? It's equally true for the "face" of your business. And remember, your clients will most likely see your business card, your website or an advertisement long before they lay eyes on you personally. You want to be certain those things look as professional as you do.

Your Business Logo

First things first. Take an honest look at your logo. (Don't have one? More on that in a minute!) Your logo is the foundation of all of your marketing material. Make certain it works for you… and then use it on everything. And I do mean everything. Repetitive use of your logo is what branding is all about. It builds recognition.

Does your logo look professional? Does it explain your business at a glance while being memorable? Do the colors represent you well? For example, primary colors (red, blue, yellow) may be eye-catching, but they can also sway the reader to think about child daycares or early education and not associate your logo with pet sitting. Take a minute to review an assortment of logos. Determine if the logos you found best demonstrate the businesses they represent. If not, why not? Now apply that thinking to your own logo.

Now, if you don't have a logo, run... don't walk... to have one created! If your logo doesn't "pop," it's time to revise it. While there are countless templates and clip arts that you can use, so can everyone else! Remember, your logo is the foundation of your marketing. It's wise to invest in it. You'll easily recoup the money you spend by having your logo professionally created. It's your image. A professional logo draws clients; an amateurish one does not.

To start, review your competition. Find five logos that you like and that you think draw attention... the right attention. Jot notes about what you really like about each one. Conversely, if you see something you dislike, make a note of that too. This information can be shared with your graphic artist to help explain the "look and feel" you're after. As they say, a picture's worth a thousand words. This sort of communication speeds the process and is invaluable to your designer.

Business Cards

Once you have your logo, don't overlook getting business cards printed. Despite the rise of the Internet and online marketing, that little 3.5 by 2-inch card comes in very handy. And people still expect to get them!

Your logo and your contact information should be front-and-center on your card. I don't mean that they should be, in fact, centered on the card, but they should be the predominant features. Company name and phone number should be largest type or the boldest typeface. People use business cards to contact you, so make it easy for them to find what they're looking for. You should also include your services. Don't assume your prospects will be aware of everything you offer.

Full-color business cards certainly draw attention, but if your budget doesn't allow for it, one or two colors plus black work as well. Don't skimp on the card stock. Choose a heavy, high-quality card stock. Even a full-color card printed on flimsy paper seems... well, cheap. Your business card should reflect your professionalism.

Since business cards aren't very big, keep it simple! Clear, concise information is best. Include only what's important. For example, customers need to know your phone number, but may not need to know your address. Don't take up valuable "real estate" on your card with unnecessary information.

When you get your cards printed, consider printing a second version for referrals or simply include the referral information on the reverse side. Include "Referred by _____" and give them to happy clients. Explain that if they give the card to a friend or family member and you get a new client because of the referral, they'll get a discount on future services. You can also give these cards to your staff members and give your staff members ten percent of the total first bill from the clients they refer.

Once you have your business cards, never... ever... go anywhere without them! You can also purchase business card-sized magnets to convert your cards into refrigerator magnets or you can have your cards designed on light-weigh magnets. Once you have magnets, you can hand those out to clients... or attach them to their refrigerators with a "welcome home" note!

Website

It's time to revamp your website if you don't completely love it. Why? If you don't love your site, then your prospects and clients certainly are not going to love it. And if they don't love it, they won't spend time on it. If they don't spend time on it, they will not be calling you.

Before you decide to overhaul your site because you're no longer in love with it and because that first impression of having your company out there for the world to see has worn off, I encourage you to ask other business owners or friends what they think of it. It may be simply that you've seen it so often, you've grown tired of it. Ask for honest feedback. Let them know you are willing to accept constructive criticism and glowing praise. Maybe it's great... or maybe it's not.

We may often think our website looks great when it doesn't look quite up to par or look as great as it could. It's a bit like living in the same house for a long time -- we don't always realize that our house looks dumpy because we see it day after day. If you don't have an office that clients visit, then your website is your business's physical presence. Be willing to clean up your website, so clients want to spend some time there to check out your business and ultimately call you to hire you.

How to Create or Revamp Your Website So It Compels Clients to Contact You:

1. Find ten pet sitting websites that you really like.

2. Write down the URL and one sentence about what draws you to each of them. For example: www.112abcpetsitter.com – the colors and copy are great! Or, www.345098petsitting.com – I like the layout of the pictures on the testimonial page.

3. Decide what qualities of the 10 sites above you want on *your* site. The layout, the graphics, photos and colors, the copy... or all the whole combination.

4. Share this information with your web designer. It will expedite the process of creating or re-designing your site, and you can avoid costly revisions.

5. *Warning: Do NOT copy anything from another website for use on your site verbatim, especially text, without written permission from the website owner. It amounts to plagiarism, possibly infringes on the owner's copyright protection and it lessens search engine optimization... yours and theirs.*

Protecting Your Website:

You certainly don't want to copy from another website, but what about someone copying your website? I've had that happen, and it's very frustrating when someone else steals your words and creative ideas. Here's how you can monitor your site for plagiarism and what to do about it if you find someone else using your copy verbatim:

1. **Go to www.Copyscape.com, select a warning banner and place it at the bottom of all the web pages that you want to protect against web copy theft.** Even though I have this banner at the bottom of my pet sitting business website, I still get pet sitters who copy my text. However, fewer do that now that I have the banner in place. Add this to your site as soon as possible

2. **Enter your website address into Copyscape's search bar to search for copies of your text on other sites.**

3. **If someone copied your text, send them this e-mail:**

Dear _____
I noticed that you have copied the text from my pet sitting website on your home page (or whatever page was copied). Please change your text immediately. Having the same copy on your site reduces BOTH of our rankings on search engines, and it's illegal. Please e-mail me to confirm that you've made the changes by_____ (a week from the date of the e-mail). Failure to do so will result in legal action.

Thank you,
Your Name
Your Business Name
Your Business Website

4. **If you need to take legal action, you can search for "Prepaid Legal Services" online.** Prepaid legal services are available in most states and offer inexpensive legal service for $30 to $40 per month.

   Prepaid legal services will draw up a 'cease and desist letter' and mail it to the party that has copied your site. If this doesn't resolve the matter, you can retain legal counsel at a discounted rate for attorney fees. You can cancel the monthly membership after the issue is resolved and start it up again when/if you need additional legal services. Using a prepaid legal service is a very cost-effective solution for pet sitters needing to resolve this and other legal matters.

5. **Check Copyscape every couple of months to ensure your text is not being copied.** Again, this will protect your search engine optimization ranking as well as your text.

Backing up Your Website:

Your web host will keep a copy of your website; however, it is still important to have your web master keep a copy of your website as well. This way, in the event of your web host crashing, your website will be protected.

For an inexpensive online backup service, visit www.mozy.com

A Word about Website Domain Names:

If you have not yet purchased a domain name, as I recommended earlier in the book, make sure to purchase a ".com" account rather than a URL that ends in ".biz" or ".net" or any other variation. Clients are more apt to remember ".com" because they've been conditioned to do so. Therefore, they will remember your site or find it more easily.

Don't forget what I shared with you earlier regarding choosing your business name wisely and carefully. If you anticipate growing, don't pick a domain name that limits you in to a specific city. Just like in choosing your business name, be sure to look ahead to get a domain name that will grow as your business grows.

Action Step

Ask at least five friends for honest feedback about whether or not they like your promotional materials. Be willing to make changes to your existing promotional items. These items are the way clients view your business. Make certain all of your promotional materials look professional. Be willing to spend money to create a quality logo, business card and website. Doing this will pay for itself many times over!

Action Step

If you don't have a website, it is crucial that you get one up as soon as possible. See the six-figure tip above if you need a webmaster to help you create a website.

Action Step

Check out the following vendors for marketing must haves, discounts and great ideas!

Great place to find LOGO creators inexpensively: Find a great new logo or make yours look even better. Go to: www.elance.com or www.guru.com.

Webhosting: The best and one of the most inexpensive web hosting companies on the market today. This hosting company also allows you to go behind the scenes and see how people find you online!

http://www.bluehost.com/track/sixfigure

Please contact the actual company, rather than Six-Figure Pet Sitting Academy™ if you have an issue with one of the products/services above. Thanks!

TEN

Get Pet Sitting Clients NOW:

Marketing and Selling that Generates Results

*"Marketing is not an event, but a process ...
It has a beginning, a middle, but never an end, for it is a
process. You improve it, perfect it, change it, even pause it.
But you never stop it completely."*

—Konosuke Matsushita, founder of Panasonic

The first step to developing a powerful marketing strategy for your business is to track what is actually generating clients and what is not generating clients. I talk to many pet sitters each week who are spending a lot of money on many different forms of marketing, but when I ask them which marketing forms are actually generating the phone calls, I will often get silence or a vague answer like 'my website.'

Before you spend a single dime on marketing, you must have a plan to track what's working. Without that, any success may be accidental. Accidental successes can't be replicated, and in order to leverage your efforts to create a six-figure pet sitting business, you must be able to repeat your success. Create a weekly tracking system where you note where your new client calls are coming from. You can create a simple Excel spreadsheet. It doesn't need to be fancy; you just need to know how many leads you are getting from different marketing streams.

Most pet sitting administration software systems allow you to track where your leads come from. Use it! However, not all of them track on a weekly or monthly basis, and I've found that tracking on a weekly or monthly basis keeps you tapped in to what's working and what's not.

When clients say "I found you online," ask them: "Do you remember what you typed in to find me?" Get more information and track how people are finding you online. It may be from a pet sitting directory that you've listed your business in or pay-per-click ads (which are called 'sponsored links' on Google). The bottom line is: You must ask!

While the majority of prospects are beginning their searches on the Internet, it's important to have a diverse marketing strategy. Cast the marketing net wide. And that's easy to do because there are many ways to market your pet sitting business. Successful marketing develops a cumulative effect – the results increase over a period of time. Having a variety of marketing strategies is crucial to get an influx of new clients.

There's no silver bullet for marketing. I can't tell you exactly what will work for your pet sitting business and what will not. Every business is different, and every geographic region is different. To be successful, you will need to experiment with a number of different strategies to find out what works best for your business. And the only way to truly know is to measure your results. While I can't proclaim what will work, I can tell you that you should never launch a campaign without knowing how you are going to track the results. You can ask pet groomers and veterinarians what marketing works for them. You're not competing with them, but you are targeting the same audience. Their advice can save you a lot of time and money.

Here's an example of an easy way to track your marketing efforts and results along with some sample entries:

WHAT?	HOW OFTEN?	COST?	AVG. REFERRALS PER MONTH?
Yellow Pages	*Annual ad*	*$160 / month*	*3 per month*
Drop off cards	4-6/weeks	Free	2 per month
Having website search engine optimized	1x every 6 months	$395	16 per month
Pay-per-click ads	Every month	Average: $55 / month	11 per month
Newspaper ad	Every week for 3 months	$68 / week	5 per month
Client referrals	Send newsletter out monthly reminding clients to refer their friends	Free	12 per month
Vinyl signs on business car windows	Once	$148 / 1x fee	7 per month
Total →		Marketing cost this month: $1030 (Pet sitters: please note that some of the expenses above are only one-time expenses and you would mark 'free' on future month's marketing tallies.	Referrals this month: 56 referrals

You may also want to consider adding code numbers or identifiers to marketing materials. This is especially true of any print marketing or advertising you do. You can ask prospects for the code number in order to help you track where they are finding out about you.

A lot of pet sitters that I coach ask me how much should they should spend on marketing. The answer really depends on what you want your pet sitting company wants to accomplish - what marketing goals and objectives you are seeking to achieve. If you are a new pet sitting business, then obviously marketing costs will be higher than if you've been in business for years. You'll have to invest more to create your own brand recognition. The good news is, it gets easier and becomes more cost effective the longer you are in business.

There is something called the 'snowball effect' for a lot of businesses. For most, once they've reached their fifth, sixth or seventh year, they find they can usually lower their marketing costs significantly. After a few years, most companies have a solid client base that provides great word-of-mouth advertising for them by recommending their service to friends and family.

If you have an older pet sitting business and are not generating at least two or three new client calls a week, then you will need to remind prospective clients about you. Somehow you've slipped under the radar! You will need to employ many of the marketing tips and tools I'll address in this chapter in order to get those new clients calls to call. More good news: Most of the options I write about in this book are low-cost methods to get your business phone to ring.

Internet Marketing

I'll start with the Internet as it really is the backbone to today's marketing. It's also one of the most inexpensive forms of marketing available. If you market your website properly online, the Internet will generate powerful results that *will* cause your phone to ring!

If you have a website, you are that much closer to getting clients right now. If you don't have a website, I recommend that you stop reading right now and begin taking steps to get a professional website created. You simply cannot have a successful business these days without a website. You'll need to make an up-front investment to create a professional website, and you may need to learn how to add content and blog posts in the future or hire a web programmer to update your site as you need to, but ultimately, a website is one of the most powerful and inexpensive ways to market your business. Simply put, you must have a website if you want to generate a six-figure business.

Improving Your Ranking

Search Engine Optimization (also called SEO) is the single most effective marketing tool online today. You will rank higher on Google and other search engines if your site is properly optimized. What does that really mean? It means that search engines connect your site to your prospective clients' queries and searches. For example, if a client types "pet sitting services in Bakerfield" into a search engine, the owner of Bakerfield Pet Sitting would certainly want to have her result show up at the top of the list. It's not guaranteed to happen unless her site is properly optimized. SEO is a big marketing tool that generates the most dollars.

So how do you improve your site by optimizing it? There are two major ways to boost your online presence and help your website populate higher on the search engine results page.

Links

Search engines like links. In fact, about 25 percent of your ranking is based on the number of links your site has. Search engines gravitate toward sites with lots of links pointed at them; it makes your site more noticeable to them. If search engines could talk they would say: "Wow, you must be an important website since you are listed on so many more websites than your competition!"

SEARCH ENGINES LOVE LINKS. GET LISTED ON OTHER WEBSITES!

When referring to links, it's important to note the difference between one-way links and reciprocal links.

One-way links occur when your business is listed on a website without having to list that particular link on your site. For example, BakerfieldPetSit.com is listed on PetsRUs.com, but PetsRUs.com is *not* listed on BakerfieldPetSit.com. That would be a one-way link for Bakerfield Pet Sitting. Reciprocal links are just that: You list a website's link on your site and in exchange they list you on theirs. Reciprocal links do boost your search engine ranking, but not as much as one-way links. In fact, some search engines look for commonality between reciprocal links. If it doesn't exist, (i.e. if your pet business has a reciprocal link with your auto mechanic), these particular links do nothing for SEO.

Listing your business on various websites and pet directories will boost your search engine ranking right away. Many pet business websites offer free listings and this is a powerful marketing tool that will get you started on your marketing campaign to get clients now!

One-way links can also be found by typing in your city and 'pet sitting' or your city and 'dog walking' as a search query. See where other sitters are listed. Clicking on the links where your competition is listed may lead you to free or low-cost directories where you can list your pet sitting business as well.

For low-cost directories that rank high in the search engines, I recommend listing your business on:

www.petsitUSA.com

www.petsitterportal.com

www.doggeek.com

www.catgeek.com

List your business on as many free and inexpensive websites as possible and watch yourself rank higher on the search engines! After listing your business on these sites, you may find that your business comes up on page one if there isn't a lot of competition for pet sitters and dog walkers in your area.

Putting a links page on your website can also help your ranking and help grow your business. A links page on your website can be a powerful marketing tool. Here's how to use your links page effectively and in a way that will generate business for your company:

Rather than calling your links page simply 'Links' as a lot of pet sitters do, I prefer to call it Pet Resources. I think resources sounds more helpful to clients. And it is! If you don't already have a links or resources page, get one created on your website.

Once you have created one, send a mass e-mail out to every local pet business (including groomers, vets, and pet stores). Offer to do a link exchange with every local pet business that will list you on their site. If you know how many "hits" you get on your website per month, let the pet businesses know. This will lead to more local reciprocal links.

It will also help you rank higher on the search engines. Why? Because when pet owners are looking for a vet, groomer or pet store, your website will come up because you have those pet businesses listed on your links or Pet Resources page.

Search Engine Optimization (SEO)

The second way to boost your search engine ranking is to have your website Search Engine Optimized (SEO). SEO encompasses 75 percent of what search engines review, or 'look at,' in order to rank pages.

Having your website search engine optimized is crucial in today's market. What's amazing is that few pet sitters are doing SEO for their sites, so if your site is search engine optimized you will often find that you will leap high above your competition on the search engines, and that will result in a massive amount of new client calls as so many people are searching for pet sitters online these days.

Search engine optimization includes key words that are strategically placed on specific locations on your website and behind the scenes which boost your search engine ranking substantially.

Most pet sitters will have to get a Search Engine Optimization (SEO) lesson to learn the ins and outs of keywords and metatags/metadata. It's important to choose the correct terms and keywords in order to come up on page one or higher on page one than you currently may be. Always remember to include geographic references in your keyword list too.

Pay-Per-Click Ads

Some search engines will pay you to allow ads to appear on your site (for example, Google AdSense). I don't recommend using Pay-Per-Click (also called PPC) ads from other companies on _your_ website. Some of my coaching clients put these ads on their website to make a few extra dollars, and they ended up having their competitors' PPC ads come up! There are also a lot of inappropriate ads that can come up and turn clients off if you decide to allow this type of advertising on your site.

The other type of PPC consists of your placing ads that appear on search engine pages (for example, Google AdWords). As far as using Pay-Per-Click to market your business: Most pet sitters find when they have their website properly search engine optimized, they do not need to spend the money for pay-per-click ads which are often very expensive to use to advertise your pet sitting service on Google or other search engines. You may find that also.

When a website has proper SEO, that website will naturally rank high on the search engine result pages (called organic ranking) within six to eight weeks of that website being optimized. You can opt for PPC if you want to add to your marketing expense; however, if you are choosing between SEO and PPC, choose SEO. SEO is more cost-effective and has longer lasting results. With most SEO, one session will suffice and within a few weeks, your site will be coming up much higher on the search engines than it did prior to being optimized.

Listing Your Business on Google Maps

If you are not already on Google Maps, simply "google" 'Google Maps' and follow the prompts to list your business. Make sure to add your logo as well as enter the keywords "pet sitting" and "dog walking" in the spot that is specifically for keywords. Putting the keywords "pet sitting" and "dog walking" in your business name for Google Maps will help you rank higher on the search engine on Google Maps. If your business name is Sweet Pea Pet Care you would then type your business as Sweet Pea Pet Sitting and Dog Walking when you list your business on Google Maps.

After listing your business on a site like Google Maps as well as other free sites, you may find that your business ranks on page one, but only if you don't have a lot of competition. However, as I previously mentioned, most of you will have to actually get your website Search Engine Optimized (SEO) to get your website's keywords and metatags listed with the correct terms and words in order to come up on page one or higher on page one than you may currently be.

Using Social Media to Boost your Online Presence

Do you know a tweet from a blog post? How about a LinkedIn connection from a Twitter follower? If not, it's time to learn what they are and how to use them to make more money in your business. Knowing how to put social media tools like Twitter, Facebook, and LinkedIn to work for your business can make a big difference in your marketing plan and can increase your revenue by thousands of dollars each month.

Savvy business owners are harnessing the power of the Internet to boost their financial bottom line, and you should too! Are YOU ready to catapult your business to success? If so, then I would encourage you to get your business listed on Twitter, Facebook, and LinkedIn today.

Twitter: http://www.Twitter.com

Facebook: http://www.Facebook.com

LinkedIn: http://www.Linkedin.com

Social media has the reputation for taking up a lot of time. Many pet sitters that I speak to about social media are concerned about having this type of marketing consume more of their valuable time.

Here are some steps that will help you set time boundaries:

- Set up a different e-mail address and link that e-mail to your social media accounts. You can create something like: socialmedia@sweetpeapetsitting.com.

- Disable the social media alerts, so you don't get an e-mail every time one of your contacts posts something.

- Make a clear list of what you want to accomplish with social media on any given day and set the timer for 20 minutes. Once the timer beeps, stop working on social media for the balance of the day.

When you post online, you may want to include photos and videos of the pets you care for, with your clients' permission of course. People love to see cute images of their pets, and they'll likely share your post with other family and friends. This can be a great source of referrals.

Blogging for Business Success

No doubt you've heard about blogs, but do you know how smart business owners are using them to gain more visibility for their businesses? Whether your blog is a stand-alone blog or part of your overall website, blogging allows you to create dynamic content that keeps people engaged. It also keeps your customers or clients coming back for more! Plus, search engines love to see fresh content. Content added to your site keeps search engines crawling. More crawling can lead to higher ranking.

With a successful blog you can:

1. Build a loyal following of clients, customers, and business prospects.

2. Become a recognized expert or leader in your field of business.

3. Easily sell your services or products to your clients.

4. Sell advertising space on your blog.

5. Build a large list of highly targeted readers.

6. Highlight specials your business is offering in order to generate immediate cash flow.

You will get the most benefit from your blog if you host the blog on your site: www.123abbpetsitter. com/blog rather than having your clients go to a separate page like Blogger or Blogspot. One of the best things about blogs is that if you have one, you will rank higher on the search engines due to keywords that are specific to the audience you want to attract. You can also partner with vets and groomers to have them write guest blog posts. This helps your blog get more exposure in the pet community as well as gives your blog variety in terms of the content. Additionally, it gives your readers useful information.

Passive Income and Blogging:

You can also create passive income with your blog! Once you have a blog, you can offer small ad space to local pet businesses. Contact veterinarians, pet groomers, dog trainers, and pet stores to ask if they would like to purchase ad space for six months or a year. Offer an introductory rate for first-time advertisers. Their blog ads will link to their websites when clicked.

You can create boxes on your blog that say "Advertise Here." When potential advertisers click on these boxes, they will be directed to your e-mail address, so they can inquire about advertising with you. You should have some website analytics about your site regarding the number of visitors, etc. each month. (The web hosting company I recommend in the prior chapter will allow you access to that data for free each day, week and month!) The more visitors you have, the more valuable this type of ad space will be. Some pet sitters make as much as $3,000 per year offering ad space to local pet business advertisers on their blogs! You can be one of them.

The Importance of Yelp Marketing

Is your business listed on Yelp?

If it isn't it should be!

Yelp has proven to be a highly effective marketing tool for pet sitting and dog walking business owners. Each day, thousands of potential clients could be searching your local Yelp site looking for a pet sitter and dog walker. Being on Yelp gives you credibility, especially if you are a new pet sitting service. If you aren't listed on Yelp, the first step you need to take to be listed is to create your business listing.

Next, you'll want to get positive Yelp reviews, and that's not difficult to do. Look at your client list. Which client consistently raves about you? Which client often refers you to their friends? Who has used you for many different pet sitting jobs over the last few years?

These are the clients to target to get five-star Yelp reviews. Send out a short e-mail to the clients you've targeted. It should read something like this:

Dear Client,

Having more Yelp reviews would be great for our business. Would you kindly take a moment to review us on Yelp? Here is the link to our business page: (Pet Sitters: be sure to include your Yelp page link here to make it easy for them to simply click and go).

Also make sure to include: *If you are not a Yelp member, it takes less than two minutes to become one.* (Letting them know that it doesn't take that long will make them more apt to sign up right then and write a review.)

And then you can end it with:

We'd really appreciate it!

Thanks,

Sally Smith
Sweet Pea Pet Sitting

Make it your goal to get at least one positive Yelp review a week. One new pet sitting company that I coached adopted this action step every week and within six months, he was so busy as a result of people finding him on Yelp that he had to hire two staff members! And that happened after only being in business for nine months!

When you get at least five excellent reviews on Yelp, you can add an icon on your home page that shows you have five (or more) Yelp reviews. This little Yelp icon adds credibility to your website and to your service.

Craigslist

Craigslist is another online spot for advertising. It's free, and many pet owners use it to find pet sitters. In order to save time, I recommend creating a "canned advertisement" that you use each week, so that you can simply cut and paste and be done. As with all marketing, track your results. If this venue does not produce any leads after several weeks, you can suspend it.

Local Marketing

I've talked a lot about Internet marketing because it is so powerful, and I want to make it clear that you really want to diversify your marketing, so that you aren't putting all your marketing eggs in one basket. That includes using a variety of Internet-based campaigns as well as local marketing as well.

To start, wear your business on yourself and your car. Do you have T-shirts with your company logo on them? Does your staff? If not, you are missing out on business. T-shirts help you promote your business and also give your company a professional image. And have one for every day of the week to ensure you always have a clean shirt to wear.

The same is true of car signs; however, they are often very controversial in the world of pet sitting. Many pet sitters ask me if having car signs on their business car is a bad idea. After all, a pet sitting sign on a car parked in front of the house basically advertises that the client is gone, right? My recommendation for using car signs is that you don't park in front of your client's house. Park down the street, and you've solved that problem of alerting potential burglars. But not without giving up your advertising.

If you don't have signs on your car, I recommend that you get them on immediately! Think about it: Your whole business is about driving back and forth to clients' homes. You could use that time and gas money to actually generate some business for yourself. If you don't have signs on your car, you are missing out on valuable and cost-effective advertising.

I recommend white vinyl signs for the back and side windows for easy viewing. You can also have your staff members advertise on their cars. Pay to have the signs put on their cars and then pay your staff member $25 to $50 per month to advertise your service on their car. It will be a worthwhile investment.

Make certain to have a contract in place that states how many months they will advertise for you and that you will be the sole advertiser on their cars. It will cost you $150 to $200 to put the signs on their cars, so you want to have an agreement of a minimum of a year. Also be certain to discuss with your staff members who are advertising your business on their cars that they are to be on their best driving behavior. Failure to do so could cause a "black eye" for your business reputation.

Why not use car magnets? They fall off or people steal them. Car magnets often get curled edges and don't look as professional as a permanent sign on the back of your car will. The only instance in which I would recommend magnets for pet sitters are for those pet sitters – you know who you are – who suffer from bursts of anger while driving or for those of you who are poor drivers. If that describes you, then by all means get magnets! You'll be better off getting magnets so you can be 'off duty' and won't be seen in a negative light. I still remember a guy from a particular pool service company that made an angry gesture at me years ago! Will I ever use that company to clean my pool? No way.

Vehicle card pockets allow you to maximize your car advertising with business cards for the outside of your car. This enables clients to take your business cards when you have it parked. I found a company that sells a water-tight quality product, and you can get 10% off some of the sturdiest business card holders available by using this link and letting them know that Six-Figure Pet Sitting Academy™ referred you: http://www.vehiclecardpockets.com. Put the code word 'GATE' in the SPECIFY field and click 'Six-Figure Pet Sitting Academy' in the drop down referral menu.

Marketing at Groomers and Vets

With all the Internet and vehicle marketing, remember to balance it with the good old-fashioned way – dropping your business cards off at your local pet stores, groomers, vets, and other pet-related businesses. Develop solid relationships with these professionals because they can be your greatest source of referrals. I recommend dropping your cards off at least every six weeks as it keeps you fresh in the mind of the local pet business owners as well as keeps your cards restocked. Professional plastic card holders can be worth the investment: stores and businesses will be more likely to display your cards or other marketing literature.

Create a marketing kit for the car in a sturdy plastic filing cabinet to make marketing easy, effortless and portable.

Have your portable marketing kit contain:

- Plastic card holders (glue your card to the front so it becomes your card holder)
- Business cards
- Glue stick
- Stapler
- Staples
- Scissors
- Index cards

- Push pins
- Log of where you've been and when

Here's a sample marketing log:

BAKERSFIELD COUNTY PET BUSINESSES			
Vet, Groomer, Pet or Feed Store	Address	Date	Comments (Declined, requested References, or Closed during regular business hours plus hard or soft card holder)
Brookline Vet. Hosp. 823-0967	900 Redwood Hwy	11/2	Hard card holder
Animal Hosp. of Brookline 823-0678	1010 Redwood Hwy	11/2	Cards kept in a binder at the front counter
Animal Kingdom Vet Hospital 823-5337	6742 Smith Road	11/2	Hard card holder
The Barking Lot 898-0562	1098 Smith Road	11/2	Soft holder on bulletin board

Print Advertising

There are many different avenues for print advertising, but there is one rule that goes for all of them: Be certain your contact information is prominent. And be sure to proofread. Double- and triple-check your phone number and website URL. It's easy to transpose digits and letters, and if you do, you've wasted your advertising budget.

Yellow Pages:

I do not recommend advertising in the hard copy yellow pages. It is very expensive and is not a very effective marketing tool. Even the *online* yellow pages directories have not been effective for most pet sitting companies.

My only exception for local yellow page advertising is for pet sitters who are in their first year of business or who live in a very small town. If this is your first year of pet sitting, then you might want to purchase a small ad in the Yellow Pages as you'll get a great 'first-time' rate, but after your first year in business, I don't recommend anything but a one-line (usually free) ad in the Yellow Pages. If you live in a small town, I recommend possibly buying a small ad on a yearly basis if it is under $30 per month and if you've talked to other business owners and they've experienced success with their yellow page ads. Any amount for marketing that is greater than $30 per month is better spent with Search Engine Optimization (SEO) or other inexpensive print advertising (see following sections).

Pet Publications:

Advertise where the pets are! Placing an ad in your local humane society newsletter or the local animal rescue organization newsletter can often generate a lot of response. These can sometimes be expensive, so try other low-cost options first before going to more costly measures to get your name out there. Call about rates to see how much this type of advertising costs in your area.

As with all your marketing efforts, keep track of how many calls you are actually getting from pet publications as this form of advertising can be one of the more expensive forms of advertising. If you are getting many clients from each ad, it will be money well spent.

Newspaper Advertising:

If you are a pet sitter who lives in a small town, you may find that advertising in your local newspaper will benefit your business. You will need to advertise for a minimum of at least three months to make it worth the money you spend advertising in a newspaper. Why? Many advertising studies have proven that potential clients need to see your ad multiple times before they will call you. Newspapers know this, so they often will offer multiple-month specials. Try it for at least three months. If you find that you are getting clients through this advertising medium, then keep going.

Writing a press release for your local newspaper will often result in free, high-profile print and online advertising. You can write a press release for any milestone in your business, not just when you are first starting up. Write a press announcing a 10-year business anniversary, adding overnight pet sitting to your list of services, expanding your service area to include the one that the newspaper serves, adding an 'expert' to your team, winning an award or getting certified in pet first aid. Remember, keep it news-oriented to improve its chance of publication. Always answer "who, what, where, when and why."(See the press release example in Chapter 2.)

You may also want to consider writing a monthly column for your local newspaper or other periodical. You can include articles about pet health and safety, dog body language, training tips and anecdotal stories. With every article, you increase your recognition as an expert in the field.

Mothers' Club Newsletters:

Mothers' club newsletters are cheap and effective. People with kids often have pets! Ads typically cost anywhere from $15 to $25 per issue and can have a readership of up to 1,000 members who read the hard copy or online newsletter.

Some mothers' club newsletters need more content and will happily write up an article about you and your business if you ask them. To find mothers' clubs in your area, simply type your city (or whatever city in which you want to increase business) and "mothers' club" into your favorite search engine.

Also consider other local publications like school newsletters and church bulletins. Many of them support themselves with advertising, and it's often very inexpensive.

Marketing through your own e-mail newsletter:

Creating your own pet sitting e-newsletter can be a simple and highly effective marketing tool to use within your existing client base. You have clients who might only use you for dog walking but who need to be reminded of all of the services you offer. Your newsletter helps you stay top-of-mind with them.

You can write articles about pet-related issues or if you are pressed for time, you can ask local vets, dog groomers, dog trainers and other pet experts to write columns for your newsletter. Having guest authors write articles for your online newsletter creates a win-win for everyone: Your clients learn valuable information, the businesses listed in your newsletter become more reputable in your clients' eyes and you save time by having others help you write the newsletter. You will also cultivate a special relationship with the vets and dog groomers that write the column.

What to include in your e-mail newsletter to make it a powerful marketing tool:

- Remind your dog walking clients that you offer pet sitting.
- Remind your pet sitting clients that you offer dog walking.
- Profile a staff member of the month and/or pet of the month.
- Offer a coupon for one free walk for new clients who are referred by a friend.
- Announce clients who have referred you and earned a bonus.
- Encourage your clients to forward the newsletter to their friends who have pets.

A monthly e-mail business newsletter can be a form of creative expression for you and an inexpensive and lucrative form of advertising for your business.

Refer me! E-mail Footer:

Here's how to use your personal e-mail to easily and effortlessly remind friends and family members to refer your service:

Put a referral reminder footer under your automatic personal e-mail signature that reads:

Referrals Welcome!
Sweet Pea Pet Sitting and Dog Walking
www.1sweetpeapet.com
555-111-0009

Postcard Marketing with Vista Print:

Vista Print offers a unique marketing service that allows you to design a postcard with your logo, and Vista Print will do target mailings to random pet owners in your zip code! Create a postcard that offers one free visit with the purchase of three to get clients in the door. Make sure to have an expiration date (three months is a good time frame) and note that the coupon is not valid over major holiday periods.

One pet sitter who tried this found that three of her clients got the postcards. So even though those clients didn't need her service (since they were already using her), she could see that this form of advertising really worked.

You can also check with your local municipality for the dog license list. If they will share that with you, you have the perfect list to which to target your marketing!

Flyers:

A lot of cities don't allow flyers to be placed on street signs or on car windshields, but if your city allows this, then I highly recommend using this form of advertising. It's simple, inexpensive and highly effective.

Create simple flyers with pull off tabs for street signs. This can be an especially good marketing technique for targeting specific areas in which you want to grow. You can also put flyers on cars that are in a pet store parking lot.

Offer one free visit with the purchase of three. As with the postcards, you'll want to add an expiration date and note that the coupon will not be valid over holidays. One pet sitter put fliers at her local Petco parking lot on a Saturday and got many calls the next week. It works!

Face-to-face Target Marketing

Pet-Friendly Apartment Buildings:

One of the most powerful marketing actions you can take as a pet sitter is to market in pet-friendly apartment buildings. Not only will you be marketing to your target audience, but you could potentially target hundreds of clients... from simply one action. *Now that is powerful marketing!*

Here's how to successfully market your business to pet-friendly apartment buildings:

- Determine which pet-friendly apartment buildings you would like to target.

- Take note of which of your current clients, if any, live at those pet-friendly apartment buildings.

- Ask those clients if you can use their name(s) in conversation and/or if they would be willing to write a letter of recommendation for you to give to the apartment manager.

- Contact the apartment manager and make an appointment to speak to him or her about how you can possibly work together.

- Dress professionally. Bring business cards to your meeting as well as the names and/or letters of recommendation from the tenants in the building.

- At the meeting, tell the building manager about your pet sitting business: How long you've been in business, what services you provide, etc.

- Offer a link on your website to advertise their pet-friendly apartment building on your Pet Resources or Links page on your website in exchange for advertising your service via an e-mail or snail mail list that the apartment manager can provide. If no such list is available, ask the manager what other means of advertising might be available to highlight your service to the building tenants.

- Create a strategic partnership. Offer a referral fee for every new client that uses your service as a result of a referral from the apartment building. This would be a good time to ask that your pet sitting service be the only pet service that they recommend.

Yappy Parties:

Some of my coaching clients have had great success with offering free "Yappy Parties" to pet friendly apartment complexes. It's a great way to introduce your business to a large pet-friendly audience by offering free treats for the dogs and wine or soda and appetizers to the humans.

To get started, simply go to the apartment building at which you are interested in hosting a Yappy Party. If you have developed a strategic partnership with a pet-friendly building, you should start with that one. If you haven't already done so, introduce yourself to the apartment manager and let him know that you would like to offer an early evening (5-7 p.m.) "happy hour" with free appetizers and beverages for humans and snacks for dogs.

One pet sitter who did this had the apartment manager contact *her* to do monthly Yappy Parties because the tenants had such a great time during the initial one. This particular pet sitter now gets a large portion of her new clients just from offering Yappy Parties!

Pet Fairs and Other Pet-Related Events:

Pet events can be expensive to participate in, but they are often worth the financial investment. Think about it: You'll be meeting a large number of prospects in a short amount of time and may come away having met many new future clients!

When you have a booth at a pet fair, make certain to have:

- A large banner so potential clients can identify you.

- Healthy dog biscuits to hand out to the dogs that pass.

- A raffle for free pet sitting service with a sign-up sheet for clients to provide their e-mail addresses and/or physical addresses so you can send them targeted marketing later either in the form of an e-mail newsletter or a postcard campaign. Plus you'll want to use their contact information to alert the winner. Ensure the raffle item is valuable enough to entice people to enter their information. You could have first, second and third prize.

- Wear your T-shirts and hats with your logo and have your staff members who are assisting wear them too.

- Fun little giveaways with your logo: your business card magnets for fridge, tennis balls or Frisbee with your logo, catnip toys with logo.

Team up with other professionals:

Realtors are often valuable resources as they are the first link between new arrivals to your area and can verbally refer you. Contact one and explore how you can work together.

You may also want to consider establishing a relationship with a travel agent. When potential clients are making vacation arrangements, they'll also need to arrange for pet care. A travel agent can quickly refer you when making reservations for his clients.

Lawn care professionals and house cleaning services are also often asked about pet sitting services. Having a relationship with these professionals can increase your referrals. You can also offer reciprocal referrals. For example, you can refer a lawn care service for your clients who will be away for extended periods of time. You may even want to consider offering this as an extra service.

The same is true for dog trainers. Exchange referrals and consider including this service to your repertoire.

Kennel clubs and cat associations are also ideal sources for leads. Research those in your area and share your information. Ask your current clients if they belong to either of these types of clubs and if you can use them as a referral/testimonial.

Networking groups:

If you consider yourself a friendly person (and not just a dog person), then networking groups can really benefit you. People will usually get a sense of whether they like you or not right away. If they like you and have pets, they will probably want to do business with you if they don't already have a pet sitter.

Business Networking International (BNI) is a networking group that has worked for a lot of pet sitters. The benefit of BNI is that it only allows one business owner within a particular profession into its group, so you will not be in a group with your competition. Also, chamber of commerce mixers can generate a lot of business and referrals from your community.

Joining or starting a pet sitters networking group can help you meet with those people who completely understand the business as well as who might be able to refer you to clients they cannot take and vice versa.

Volunteer opportunities:

You may want to volunteer at your local humane society or animal shelter. Be sure to wear your promotional shirt if they will let you. In addition to volunteering, offer your services as a raffle prize or for a charity auction for any fund-raisers that local organizations conduct. You'll have to determine what caveats you may want to place on the prize such as distance and expiration date. Also, consider sponsoring a drive to support your local SPCA or shelter. Ask each of your clients to donate pet food.

Referrals and testimonials:

As I mentioned earlier you can offer a referral fee to staff members for referring new clients. Let them know that you will pay them ten percent of the first bill from any new client they refer as a bonus.

Reward existing clients for referring new clients. Offer clients one free visit or walk or half off one overnight as a thank you when they refer you. Include a three-month expiration with the offer so that you aren't approached by clients years later.

Always ask your happy clients for a testimonial. If they send a note or e-mail extolling your great service, respond by thanking them and asking if you can share their testimonial in your marketing material and on your website. Include full names (with permission) and their towns to establish the highest credibility.

Closing the Sale

Great marketing will get your phone ringing, but you must also close the sale when speaking with clients. Set clear objectives for each sales call and sales interaction. How do you do this? Decide what exactly you want from a particular call before you begin. Is the goal to have this person become a life-long client? Is the goal to have this person easily and effortlessly say yes by scheduling a time to meet you or one of your staff members? Determine what it is you want in order to get it. If you don't have a map of where you are going, you won't know how to get there or even if you've arrived when you do!

It's also important to be clear about how many client calls you want to be converted to actual clients. 80%? 90%? By implementing the actions that follow, you should be able to convert 90 to 95 percent of your ideal client calls to YES's.

Returning Client Calls

First of all, be sure to have enough time to return client calls! A lot of pet sitters are returning calls while in the car, in between bites of their sandwich or at a pet sitting job. This leads to impatience and a harried quality to the call which can turn clients off. Being in a hurry or being impatient does not lead to high sales!

How you can avoid being in a hurry with clients on the phone?

Set aside three specific times in which you will return calls: 8:00/2:00/6:00. You can even let clients know on your voicemail when you will be returning client calls that day and ask them to leave the best number at which to reach them during one of those three times.

Take a deep breath and really relax before dialing the phone. Your initial phone conversation can set the stage for a long-term lucrative relationship, or it can derail your efforts if you're uptight, rushed or uninterested in speaking to a prospective client. Your mood comes through in your voice no matter which words you use.

Realize there is a person on the other end of the phone. It's someone who took the time to call you rather than calling another pet sitter. This person deserves all of your attention at that moment. Give it to them. Never multi-task while returning client calls as clients will hear your inattention in your voice.

If you happen to field a call when you know you don't have the proper time to dedicate to it, let the prospect know and ask for a mutually agreeable time to return the call.

Have complete confidence in yourself and your staff.

Without complete confidence, you will not be able to "sell" yourself or your staff. If you don't believe that the people who work for you will do a good job, then they shouldn't be working for you. I'll be covering how to hire the best people in the next chapter.

Focus on relationships and not transactions.

It's important to establish trust with your clients. Once you do, you will have a client for the life of your business. When pets die, you will be the only one your clients will think of when they get a new pet. Remember that the first phone call with a new client is especially about creating a connection and cultivating a relationship, not trying to 'sell' them something.

Listen first, then explain what it is you do.

Ask them what it is they are looking for and then listen. Don't interrupt. Take notes as they share dates of travel, service needed, etc. When they are finished, explain clearly and concisely what your services entail. For example, "Our cat sitting visits are 30 minutes and include feeding the kitty, bringing in the mail and the newspaper, watering a small number of plants and scooping the litter daily."

> **ONE OF THE BEST WAYS TO CLOSE THE DEAL IS TO MAKE IT EASY FOR YOUR CLIENTS TO DO BUSINESS WITH YOU!**

Establish the value of your pet sitting service before you quote price.

This can include stating how long you've been in business and how you want to help them. "We've been in business for 8 years, and as the owner, I'm personally committed to providing you with the highest quality care. For a 30-minute cat, visit we charge $25."

Make it easy for the client to use your service.

How do you do this? By smoothly suggesting a time to have the client meet one of your wonderful staff members. Ask them for three dates and times when they can meet you or one of your staff members.

Having trouble closing the deal with potential clients that call? Using this script below can have you closing the deal nearly every time (or at least get them to meet with you where you can then close the deal).

How to Close the Deal on the Phone:

Ring! Ring!

Pet Sitter: Hello and thanks for calling Sweet Pea Pet Sitting. This is Jennifer. How may I help you?

Caller: Hi Jennifer, this is Sharon. I'm calling to see if you are available for pet sitting?

Pet Sitter: Hi Sharon, thanks for calling. Yes, I'm definitely available. What are your dates?

Caller: Our dates are June 1 to June 6. How much do you charge?

Pet Sitter: Sure, I'd love to help you with that. Before I quote you a price can you please tell me what kind of animals do you have?

Caller: We have two dogs and a cat.

Pet Sitter: Okay, great. Do you want overnights or pet visits?

Caller: We'd like to compare prices to see which service we'd like to go with.

Pet Sitter: No problem, I can give you rates for both of our services. For overnights for two dogs and a cat it will be $75/night. For visits it will be $30 per 45-minute visit.

Our overnight service includes two walks: one in the morning, one in the evening, feeding the animals, scooping the litter, watering plants if necessary and bringing in the mail and newspaper and of course, staying overnight in your home. We provide the same services during a visit, of course with the exception of spending the night. Which would you prefer: overnights or visits?

Caller: Overnights.

Pet Sitter: Would you like me to go ahead and gather your information so I can set up a time to meet with you?

(Notice how Jennifer moved right into setting up the interview in order to close the deal? The mistake a lot of pet sitters make is pausing too long after stating the price due to their own discomfort regarding asking for money or feeling like the client might reject them. If there is too long of a pause from the pet sitter after the price is announced, the client may find herself a little unsure about proceeding. Hesitancy on the part of the pet sitter often indicates a lack of confidence. Moving to the next step – asking for the appointment – shows you have confidence in your business. It's a quality your prospects want in their pet sitter!)

Now at this point the client may say, "Whoa! What a minute here! That will be X amount of dollars for X number of overnights. That's too much."

That's when our pet sitter skillfully presents options.

Pet Sitter: We can do visits instead if you like. That will only be (reaching for a calculator or looking at price list on office wall) $60 per day for two visits instead of $75/night. Will that work for you? (Notice how the pet sitter keeps putting the ball in the client's court to have the client move this conversation along.)

Client: I still think that's too much. I can't afford that.

Pet Sitter: (kindly and gently) I hear that you say that you think you can't afford that and I just want to let you know that most kennels would charge X amount of dollars, so we are actually less than a kennel would be (or only a little more). And one of the many benefits of hiring us is that we come to you.

Client: Well, you have a point there.

Pet Sitter: And we've been in business for 2 years, and as the owner I am committed to providing you with a great experience. I know you'll be happy with the care I <or we'll> provide for your animals.

Would you like me to get your information now so I can set up a time to have one of our sitters meet with you?

Client: Sure.

It just takes a little tenacity and willingness to go past the "no" to get to the "yes." Most of the time, if you keep explaining the benefits of your service, you will win that client over. Don't be a jerk or give a hard-sell about it, but be confident in your price and the service you provide and most of the time you will be able to easily and effortlessly close the deal even if a client says no in the beginning!

And remember: People act because of emotion… not logic. When you reassure clients that they will have a stress-free experience in working with you, you create a positive emotion – one they'll act on.

How to Close the Deal in Person: The Client Interview:

I'm often asked by my new staff and coaching clients alike: "What should I wear to the client interview?"

You want to wear nice clothes but not *too* nice. After all, you should be interacting with the pet, and your clients will not expect you to be dressed to the nines. Simply dress and act professionally. Clean jeans and your company t-shirt are fine.

During the initial phone conversation, some new clients may say that a personal interview is unnecessary. Insist on a personal interview prior to the sit. Why? The dog may not be friendly, and you want to know that while the owner is present. Plus it's important to have the client review the locations of the items you'll be needing to care for their pets and home while they are away.

Also be sure to remember that clients want to see you connect with their pet(s); that's why they hired you. So don't be afraid to get on the ground and connect to the pet at the pet's level. Clients love this and the pets do too!

Be warm and friendly while maintaining a professional and competent manner. If you are shy (many pet sitters feel more comfortable around animals than people), I suggest carrying a clipboard. It helps create a bit of a boundary, which may help you feel more comfortable and 'safe', and you can position it to help shield the notes you take during the interview.

Never leave without a signed contract and the key. And personally check to see that the key works. Ask who else has permission to be on the property while your client is away. Neighbors? Adult children? Make notes about the pet's behavior during the initial interview, so that you'll recognize unusual ones once the animal is in your care.

Record-keeping of client and pet details is critical to your success. Vital information that you should gather and maintain includes:

- Client's name and address; assorted phone numbers (home, work, cell) and special items to be aware of about the house.

- Pet names, breeds and ages. Also keep their characteristics, allergies, medical conditions and particular behaviors on file.

- Type of service (and number of visits/walks per day) and any special requirements needed.

- Pets' immunization information and expiration dates. Also, any required medication. Insist on having proof of immunizations. You visit a lot of pets, so it's important for their safety and for yours.

- Client's veterinary clinic, phone number, address and directions.

- Emergency contact information (who can be contacted if the client is unavailable).

- Location of supplies and types of pet food.

Be certain to keep any security information, such as keypad entry codes, secure and separate from house keys. Also, collect information about who to contact in case of a household or property emergency, such as the plumber or a handy-man. You'll know who to contact in case you arrive to find the water heater leaking, and your clients will appreciate your professionalism.

Create an emergency plan for weather-related catastrophes. Review it with clients, stressing the importance of having emergency contact information. It shows clients that you're well-prepared and professional.

Maintain digital photos of the pets in your database. You never know when you may need to reference it in an emergency. Clearly state in your contract how veterinary emergencies will be handled and how they will be paid.

Carry your signed contract with you when you go that particular home and create I.D. cards for yourself and your staff members. Both items will help prove you have permission to be in the house or on the property should you need to. It's not unheard of for the police to stop by based on a call from neighbors or as part of a routine vacation check if your client has requested that service.

If you have permission to walk a client's dog off leash, it is important to always create temporary I.D. tags for those pets that includes your contact information ("This pet is being cared for by….").

At the end of the client interview, be sure to collect payment or give clients an invoice and ask that they mail their payment or give you their credit card information at least five days prior to departure. Waiting for clients to send a check until after they've returned from a trip will inhibit your cash flow. If new clients are concerned about your getting paid prior to their departure for services not yet rendered, let them know they can write a post-dated check and have them date it for their return date.

Action Step

List your business on Twitter, Facebook and LinkedIn. Begin making connections with clients and other pet related businesses!

Stick to clear time boundaries (15-30 minutes a day) so social media creates more business for you instead of wasting your time.

Action Step

Find out how high you rank on Google and the other search engines by typing in your town and the words 'pet sitting.' If you are sixth on the page or lower, get a search engine optimization coaching session with the Six-Figure Pet Sitting Academy™ or another company that can help you rank higher on search engine optimization. Here is the link for the Six-Figure Pet Sitting Academy's™ SEO coaching page:

*http://www.sixfigurepetsittingacademy.com/PetSitterSearchEngine
Optimization.html*

Action Step

*In addition to dropping your cards of at various pet businesses you
can have your car work for you when your car is parked! How?
Purchase business card holders for the outside of your car:
http://www.vehiclecardpockets.com*

*SAVE 10% on your order by selecting 'Six-Figure Pet Sitting Academy'
from the WHERE DID YOU HEAR ABOUT US drop down menu. Put
the code word 'GATE' in the SPECIFY field. You will receive a 10%
discount on your cards by entering that code.*

Action Step

*List your business on Google Maps as well as on the free and low-cost
sites listed in this chapter. Be sure to add "Pet Sitting and Dog
Walking" after your business name even if your business name doesn't
contain those words as part of your legal business name. Sweet Pea Pet
Care would become Sweet Pea Pet Sitting and Dog Walking. Doing this
will cause you to rank higher on Google Maps!*

Action Step

*Create your own e-mail newsletter. E-mail newsletters are a great way
to market to prospects and stay "top-of-mind" with the pet sitting client
contacts you already have.*

Action Step

*Do local marketing to promote your business. Put your business
information on your car by getting signs professionally placed on your
windows or magnet signs on your car doors. Create a marketing kit
for your car. Drop off cards at your local vet, groomer and pet store.*

Be willing to be seen and to speak to merchants while taking action to promote your business. Include a footer in your personal e-mail account that advertises your business in a subtle way.

Action Step

Find out what publications are in your area and advertise in them. Investigate mothers' club newsletters and advertise in them. Try Vista Print Targeted Marketing at www.VistaPrint.com.

Action Step

Meet potential clients face-to-face by creating your own Yappy Party or sign up to have a booth at a pet fair. Look online for inexpensive giveaways like catnip balls and dog toys with your logo on them.

Action Step

Practice your selling technique with at least two friends this week. Try different ways of selling your service without being pushy. Get feedback from friends about how you came across to them.

Action Step

Put a clearly defined rate sheet on your office wall, so that when clients call you can glance at your rate sheet to say the rate quickly and full of confidence.

ELEVEN

You, the Employer:

Secrets to Finding, Working with, and Keeping Good Staff Members

*"I hire people brighter than me
and then I get out of their way."*

–Lee Iacocca

If you are against hiring people to help you in your pet sitting business, I want to let you know right off the bat that it will be challenging, if not impossible, to create a six-figure pet sitting without hiring the staff to support you.

If you have fear and trepidation about hiring pet sitters to work for you realize that you are normal... so welcome to the club! Everyone that is new to hiring pet sitters in their pet sitting business feels nervous and often very anxious before they hire. I did. But I pushed past my fear because I knew that I could not run the kind of successful business that I wanted to create without hiring people to work for me.

Why?

Because I am only one person. I can't do it all.

And more importantly, *I don't want to do it all.* In fact, when I set my goal to run my business differently, I discovered a simple truth that set me free. That truth was: Though I LOVE animals and though I started this business out of my deep and utter love for animals, I got a little tired of caring for animals seven days a week.

I realized that:

- I wanted to have time for myself.
- I wanted to have the option of not working if/when I didn't want to.
- I wanted to be able to work *on* my business instead of always *in* my business.
- I wanted to be able to stay at home in bed if I was sick.
- I wanted to be able to go on vacation *and make money while I was away.*

When I discussed commitment earlier in this book and suggested that you would have to dedicate yourself entirely to your business for a year (or for the time frame you felt was appropriate for you in order to create business success), I did not mean that you can't delegate some of your pet sitting to some people who can help you. It will very likely be impossible to grow your business without doing so.

Here's what you want to consider before hiring:

1. Figure out the holes/gaps in your schedule, so you will know what you need.

2. If you are hiring because *you* need time off (and not just because you are getting more calls than you can handle), then figure out your ideal schedule compared to what you are currently working. Knowing that information will allow you to identify those gaps, so you can fill them.

Unless you are completely burned out, change your schedule slowly. Take Mondays off from dog walking and keep your Tuesday through Friday walks, or take T/TH off and keep M/W/F. This will help clients adjust too as well as making a smooth financial transition for your business as you shift from you doing all the work to paying your staff to do it.

Once you've decided what you want (dog walker) when (T/TH) and where (a particular town or county), it's time to use a crucial hiring tool for pet sitters called the Application Packet for Pet Sitters and Dog Walkers™.

You can create this packet for your business, or to save time and effort, you can buy an already developed application packet from the Six-Figure Pet Sitting Academy™ website, so you don't have to reinvent the wheel. This packet was invented by me in 1997, and it has made hiring so easy that I wouldn't (and haven't) hired pet sitters and dog walkers without it since creating it years ago.

Here's what the Application Packet for Pet Sitters and Dog Walkers™ contains, what it does and why it is one of the most important items required to hire great people:

1. Cover sheet explaining that applicants will need to fill out this packet and <u>mail</u> it back to you.

2. Job descriptions and pay rates for each job. The three job descriptions that are enclosed in my packet: dog walker, overnight pet sitter, am/pm pet visitor.

3. Basic application standard to any job.

4. Application specific to pet sitting with pet sitting related questions.

5. Walk schedule: See at a glance when this person is available or not available to make sure it matches your needs and see areas they are available to cover.

6. Pet sitter schedule: See dates for which they are already booked, holidays that they are available for, and areas that they are willing to cover.

Once you have your application packet ready, you'll want to go ahead and place an ad on Craigslist. My experience has been that Craigslist is the best place to advertise for help. Why? You get a vast pool of people to consider. Don't worry about getting too many applicants. Your Application Packet for Pet Sitters and Dog Walkers™ will help weed the bad applicants out and bring the good applicants to your attention.

Post your ad in the employment category on Craigslist under etc. jobs, P/T jobs and/or under domestic under the category 'gigs.' Please note there in some cities Craigslist charges a fee for job ads but not for 'gigs' ads. You will probably get more responses under "etc. jobs" so post there first.

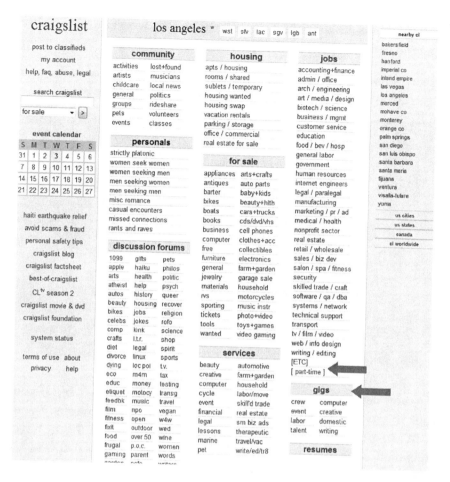

In addition to placing an ad on Craigslist you can also consider asking your local Humane Society or animal shelter about its volunteers. Maybe one of them is looking for a pet sitting job. You may also find another pet sitter who's interested in working for someone else rather than running her own business, especially one who finds the administrative and marketing side of the business to be too challenging.

Be very clear in your ad about exactly what you need: (dog walker) where (what city?) and when (T/TH, between the hours of 11 a.m. and 2 p.m.). You also want to spell out the pay rate in your ad as well as clearly stating that this is a very part-time job. I pay my staff 50 percent of what I charge clients. If you are paying too much, you won't make a profit; if too little, then you won't attract quality people to work for you.

Okay, so now your ad is up, and you are getting responses. The first step is to weed out the ones who seem unsuitable right away.

SIX-FIGURE SUCCESS TIP

E-mail or mail those particular applicants the Application Packet for Pet Sitters and Dog Walkers™ and have them MAIL the packet back to you.

Why have the applicants mail the packets back? It's more effort for the applicants, and therefore, you'll get a higher caliber of staff responding simply by noting who mails the packet back and who doesn't. I have noticed that if I send out ten packets, I might get five back. Of those five, typically only one or two will probably be someone I want to hire. But I've saved myself many hours by not interviewing unsuitable applicants.

Do you need to respond to everyone? It's nice if you can, but if you get 100 to 200 e-mails in response to your ad, then obviously you can't respond to everyone *and* run your business! So if you have received a large response to your ad, you need only respond to those that seem like they might be a good fit.

Review the packets at your leisure (one of the many benefits of using the application packet).

As you are reviewing the Application Packet for Pet Sitters and Dog Walkers™, it's important to really pay attention to whether they followed instructions on the packet. One question on the packet is: "List three words to describe why you would make a great pet sitter or dog walker." If they write three *sentences* to that question, they probably are not a good fit! Remember, you want someone who follows directions in written form (think about client notes and how important those are to follow!)

Of the application packets that are mailed to you, there may be a couple applicants who really stand out. You may want to "Google" the applicants to see if anything untoward about them populates on the Internet. Remember, they will be representing your company. Call those applicants who really stand out about the rest for an interview.

Face-to-face interview

Where to meet? A coffee shop or a dog park makes a good meeting place for interviewing potential staff members. Note the applicant's punctuality. If the applicant is late, consider the reason. Also, keep in mind that an interview can be stressful. A few nerves are normal, so allow the applicant a few minutes to adjust. Start with small talk to create a friendly atmosphere. Remember:

- Have dogs/cats at interview. See how they are with hyper dogs – always a good test!

- Pay attention to your initial impression.

- Review the packet with them and review their availability compared to your needs.

Ask questions like:

- What kinds of animals do you prefer caring for: dogs or cats?

- Have you ever had anything go wrong at a pet sitting or dog walking job (if they've got pet sitting references) and if so, how did you deal with it?

- What would you do if: describe scenarios like fox tails or if a dog has diarrhea?

- Do you know how to pill a cat? How do you do it?

- Do you know how to administer Sub-Q fluids? How?

- While they are answering your questions, pay attention to your own impressions in addition to their answers. How do you feel around this person? Do you feel relaxed? Your clients will too. Anxious? Your clients will too!

Often pet sitters who call me for coaching regarding the hiring process are shocked to learn that I don't ask a lot of questions of potential applicants, and here's why: Anyone can answer questions correctly! It's up to you to *discern* whether this person is actually trustworthy and able to do the job.

While they are answering your questions, also pay attention to:

- Are they personable?

You probably want to hire someone who likes animals *and* people. If applicants say "I like dogs more than people because dogs don't talk back" that's always a yellow flag for me because I need staff members who can relate well to both pets and people and put my clients at ease.

- Do they present well? Are they dressed neatly, etc.

- Do they look you in the eye when they speak?

- Do they seem confident and comfortable but not cocky?

After you've asked a few questions, you'll probably have an idea if you want to hire them or not. If they are a definite no, let them know that you have other interviews and that this is just a short interview to get to know them. Be sure to call them back in a few days and let them know you've hired someone else. Destroy their application packet and let them know you have destroyed it as it contains personal and private information on it.

If they are a good fit then go over your Welcome Packet with them which contains:

- Policy and procedure list.

- Client interview sheets.

- Checklists to do at each job.

- Contract with non-compete clause to be signed.

Background checks before hiring?

I don't do background checks, but it doesn't mean you shouldn't. I've hired so many people throughout the years that I've really learned to trust my intuition. The Application Packet for Hiring Pet Sitters and Dog Walkers™ really helps weed out the bad ones. Plus the application contains the question: Can we do a background/criminal check on you? Most everyone who answers 'yes' is going to know they have nothing to hide.

However, if you are new to hiring or you are nervous about hiring, then you <u>do</u> want to get a background check on an applicant before hiring. You should also check your insurance policy and bonding agreement. Either or both of them may require background checks. Contact NAPPS if you are a member of that pet national pet sitting organization, and they can guide you on the best background check company.

You will also have to decide if you'll hire someone as an independent contractor (IC) or an employee. They are two distinct classifications. According to the IRS, "It is critical that you, the business owner, correctly determine whether the individuals providing services are employees or independent contractors. Generally, you must withhold income taxes, withhold and pay Social Security and Medicare taxes, and pay unemployment tax on wages paid to an employee. You do not generally have to withhold or pay any taxes on payments to independent contractors."

There are pros and cons to each classification. Independent contractors require less paperwork on your part and you're off the hook when it comes to withholding taxes. ICs must be responsible to pay their own taxes. However, you cannot tell them what to do, and it's possible they'll take your clients. While you can ask them to sign a non-compete when you hire them that is not a sure-fire guarantee and can lead to a drawn out legal battle. On the other hand, employees are under your control. They may not legally take your clients, but it is generally more expensive to have employees, and they come with a lot more paperwork.

Speak with your accountant to determine which classification makes the most sense for your business. It's not a choice you should make without professional advice.

Welcome Aboard

Provide new staff members with your promotional shirts and also consider providing them with a customized bag to carry supplies, etc.

Review your policies and procedures, and your first hire means that those should be in written format and spelled out in detail. Be clear about smoking, dress code, gum chewing, door locking, and general conduct as well as how each visit should be conducted. Since you've already written your step-by-step organized approach, include that for your staff members as well. If it's a good idea for you to carry out every visit in the same way, it's a good idea for them too.

Also, review your own insurance policy to be certain you understand exactly what is… and isn't… covered regarding your staff members.

Accompanying staff members on client interviews

I recommend those business owners who are new to hiring go to at least the first three client interviews with their staff. You can do some role playing with your staff members prior to the first client interview. This will help your staff (and you) feel comfortable when they are doing the actual interview with the client. Start by having her play the role of the client with you in the role of the sitter and then reverse it.

When you are at the client interview, you can handle the initial introduction, but then allow your staff member to take charge. Have your staff member carry the clipboard containing the client interview sheet and have her ask the necessary questions of the client.

When the interview is complete and you are outside, you can debrief: Be generous with praise first and then talk about what could have been done differently (if there was anything).

After the third interview or when you and the staff member both feel comfortable, allow her to go by herself. This will save you time to put your energy into revenue-producing activities. And trying to find time to schedule three different participants for a meeting can be very challenging.

Monitoring Staff Members

Have staff members call you from the clients' home when they arrive and depart. This way you can get the date/time stamp on your business phone and can track the time that the sitter spent at each job.

Once staff has been with your company for a while, I recommend just having them call when they do their first visit or overnight and then when they do their final visit or overnight for that particular client.

You may also want to stop by the client's homes to see how things are going. Some pet sitting business owners who are very nervous about new staff do that and find it helps alleviate any fear or distrust they might have.

Client questionnaires will help you get feedback on how your new staff member is doing. It's often easier for clients to write out their feedback than pick up the phone to let you know about their experience using your new staff member. Keep it simple for them and for you! My experience has proven that clients are more apt to actually fill out and mail back a written questionnaire than they are to complete an online questionnaire, especially if you include a self-addressed stamped envelope along with your questionnaire.

SIX-FIGURE SUCCESS TIP

Always send a client questionnaire out to ALL clients, but especially new clients. Make it simple for clients to mail it back by including a self-addressed stamped envelope.

A final note about the questionnaire: Share the feedback, both positive and negative, with your staff. The positive feedback will keep your staff motivated and the negative feedback will get them back on the right track.

If clients complain about your staff member:

Call the staff member to get his side before assuming that he did something wrong. Always give him the benefit of the doubt before you've assumed the client is right. I've often found that my sitters had a good reason for doing what was perceived by the client as 'wrong.' If I had accused the sitter without having all the facts, I might be minus a good sitter and a client!

However, if a new staff member *did* do something wrong on the first, second or third job, pay attention to that. Usually people do their best on the first, second and third jobs. If a staff member is doing a poor job on the first, second or third job, she might not be the right fit for your company. Pay attention! Hiring is like dating; people prove who they are in the first few meetings. It's up to you to pay attention.

You'll save yourself stress down the road when you honestly assess the applicants in those first few minutes of meeting for the interview and how they perform in first few jobs you give them.

If staff did something wrong, honestly assess *your* role in the error.

- Did *you* leave something out in your instruction to them?
- Did you fail to educate or train your staff members properly?
- Where were you not entirely clear with them about something?

How to Keep Your Staff

Here are some tips to keep your staff happy and content and working with you for years:

- Gratitude - Express it! If you received a positive client questionnaire, read it to that person and offer thanks. Feeling appreciated is the number one reason why many people stay in jobs.

- Surprise staff members by rewarding them with a random paid day off.

- Money – Give a raise without being asked for it.

- Give unexpected gifts like massage certificates to your key people when they least expect it.

- On your website (under FAQ) or in company literature, include the statement 'tips are not expected but are appreciated' to encourage more tips from your clients.

- If you charge a holiday fee, give staff half of the holiday fee.

- Give holiday gifts - Money to your crucial staff members, coffee gift cards or bookstore gift cards to those other staff members.

Remember: Start saving now for your staff holiday gifts.

- Consider monthly staff meetings to discuss problems and solutions, marketing ideas and to share kudos from clients. (Remember the cardinal rule about managing people: Reward in public, reprimand in private.)

Action Step

If you want to hire staff and find that you are afraid of hiring people, write down all of the fears that you have that stand in the way of hiring.

Then, look at all the reasons why you DO want to hire staff members and write them down.

Compare both lists above and see if the benefits would in any way outweigh the fears that you may have. If you have fear, realize that thousands of pet sitters have and do hire people every day. You are not alone. Be willing to give up your fears to pursue your dream of having a business and a life!

Action Step

Look at this week's or next week's schedule and determine what day(s) you need to hire someone to work for you so that you can get a well-needed break.

Action Step

Determine your hiring deadline and begin breaking the hiring process down in manageable actions to begin the hiring process today.

Action Step

Create your own application packet to use as a hiring tool. Or to save time you can purchase an Application Packet for Hiring Pet Sitters and Dog Walkers™ and Welcome Packet for the New Staff Member ™ for your new staff members.

Here is the link for all of the Six-Figure Pet Sitting Academy ™ hiring tools for pet sitters including the Application Packet for Hiring Pet Sitters and Dog Walkers™ and the Welcome Packet for Pet Sitters and Dog Walkers™:

http://www.sixfigurepetsittingacademy.com/petsitter_products.html

Action Step

Be willing to look at what is not working with your staff and make changes or let difficult staff members go. Determine if any of your staff members are burned out and figure out when/how to give them a break.

Action Step

Commit to mail out client questionnaires to new clients who have used new sitters this week, so you can get honest feedback about how your new staff members are doing. Be sure to include a self-addressed stamped envelope, so it's easy for clients to mail the form back to you.

Action Step

Begin some of the other recommended suggestions for keeping your valuable business asset – your staff.

TWELVE

Client Details in a Service-Based Pet Business:

How to Provide Great Service *and* Train Your Clients on How to Treat You

*"Training your clients is like training your dog -
you have to be loving, firm and
your yes and no have to be very clear."*

–Kristin Morrison

This chapter is not about customer service. There are already so many "How to give great customer service" books out there. This book is not one of them. Instead, this chapter is about the little… and the big… details that, if left unchecked will cause the average pet sitter a decrease in revenue, sleep and peace of mind.

Don't be one of those pet sitters who experiences unnecessary anxiety and stress. Do the exercises in this book. And if you find your customer service skills lacking, then by all means get a customer service handbook. Customer service is crucial for the success of any business, and bad customer service can cause a business to fail no matter how much business knowledge you have.

I can sum up how to give great customer service to your clients in two words.

Be nice.

It really is that simple. Pet sitting is a service-based business, and it's also based on being loving. Loving with the animals, but hopefully being loving with the animals' people too.

Here is the definition of the word 'service' from the dictionary:

service [sur-vis] noun, verb

1. *an act of helpful activity; help; aid: to do someone a service.*

If you can remember that you are running a *service-based* business, the next time you answer your phone, you just might have a client for the life of your business.

Being nice means being friendly on the phone with clients and doing what can be done to help them with their pet care needs. It means paying attention to the details. It means paying attention to the droopy tomato plant in your client's yard and watering that plant... even if your client forgot to tell you to water. Being nice means leaving a warm welcome home note along with a cute story about the pet. You can also send a "reverse post card" to your clients. Snap a photo of the pet and send it to them via e-mail or text. They'll appreciate that you took the time to do something nice.

Being nice, however, does not mean being a doormat. So many people confuse being nice with being a doormat. I've coached hundreds of pet sitters who are stressed out because they feel they are being thrown around by the whims of their clients. And yet they are the one agreeing to whatever it is that their client has asked for.

Here's the thing: We train our clients how to treat us. It's exactly like dog training. Give the dog an inch, and he'll take a mile. Why? Because we've given him an inch a few times, and he realizes he can do it over and over. If you are a dog trainer in addition to being a pet sitter, you know that breaking the pattern at that point with dogs is quite difficult. Thankfully, training our clients is not quite as difficult as dog training, but it does require being firm and committed to ourselves.

Training your clients really comes down to saying no to client requests that don't work for you. Saying no in a gentle and loving way.

We train our clients how to treat us by saying no to outlandish requests that just don't work for us or charging them a "$30 last minute" fee in addition to the regular fee when they call requesting us to start a pet sitting job in an hour. We train our clients when we let them know we are not available to do an 11 p.m. visit on a Tuesday night. We train our clients that we don't pick up the phone after 7 p.m. by not answering the phone or returning calls after that hour.

We also may find ourselves training our clients by letting them go.

Bad Client, No Biscuit: Dealing with Difficult Clients

One of the biggest business epiphanies I've had happened a few years ago and completely changed the way I dealt with my clients. Let me share it with you:

I'd had a challenging phone interaction with a person who was the poster child for being a Bad Client. She was demanding, nit-picky with my staff, cheap (she had a huge fit each time I raised my prices) and was generally unhappy about the service we provided no matter how much we bent over backward to help her. This challenging phone conversation with her was one of the many I'd had with her over the years and like all the others, it left me feeling socked in the stomach and depleted for hours afterward. I realized that nothing we could do would make her happy, and that left me feeling very confused about what to do next.

Before I became a pet sitter and a business coach for pet sitters, I worked in the restaurant business where the old adage was: The Customer is Always Right.

This adage has served me well in my pet sitting business because it's helped me cultivate stellar customer service and instilled in me loving kindness toward my clients even when I'm grouchy and don't feel like being loving and kind. My clients' well-being is very important to me as is my commitment to providing them with the best pet sitting and dog walking service that I possibly can.

However, after having this phone interaction with Bad Client, I realized that only 5% of my energy was going to 95% of my 'well-behaved' clients and 95% of my energy was going to the 5% of really difficult, demanding, and nit-picky Bad Clients that I had.

Read that again, please. Let it really sink in and see how that percentage applies to your business.

Whew. That epiphany changed the way I looked at my clients from then on.

With this lightning bolt of awareness came the realization that I could actually do something about the quality of my business relationships. Here I was simply accepting that having Bad Clients was something every business must deal with and even cater to ('the customer is always right' adage), but what if this way of thinking was untrue?

NO MATTER WHAT THEY PAY YOU, "BAD CLIENTS" ARE NEVER WORTH THE STRESS THEY CAUSE. BE WILLING TO LET THEM GO!

Because dealing with the handful of difficult clients was taking up so much of my time and energy and even causing me to spend less time with the 95% of clients who were easy to work with, I decided to do some spring cleaning of my client list and let the Bad Clients go.

Here's what I did and how I did it:

1. **I looked at my client list with honest eyes and wrote down the names of the difficult clients.** As I wrote down the difficult client names, I found myself rationalizing: "Well, this one isn't so bad, they pay us $____ a month and the work really isn't that hard." I had to keep focusing on my mission: "Does having interactions with this client deplete me and cause me a lot of stress?" If so, they went on the list, despite my financial rationalizations.

2. **After writing down the 'difficult client' names, I examined whether the money they were paying us was worth the stress they were causing to me and my staff.** Have you heard the term 'golden handcuffs'? This term

applies to having well-paying but difficult clients. I had to look at the value of peace in my business, and if I was ready to commit to having a peaceful business, I had to let the truly difficult clients go. I also realized that I wanted... and was committed to having... 100% of my client base be clients I enjoyed caring for and working with.

3. **Once I decided that having a peaceful business and harmonious client relationships were worth more to me than all the money in the world, I was ready to take action.** I began to realize that I was spending a lot of money on 'self care' (massage, etc.) because I needed to reward myself after feeling emotionally beaten up by certain Bad Clients. So here I was actually spending the money that I'd made from them to take care of myself because of my depleting interactions with them! Crazy, I know, and yet I imagine you know what I'm talking about if you have any Bad Clients.

I began the process of calling the difficult clients and letting them know that we were no longer able to provide service for them. When they asked the reason, I'd say that "I just didn't think our service was a 'fit' for what they were looking for."

Some clients got angry that we were firing them. I stayed strong during the occasional emotional outburst from these clients because I'd come to the firm resolution that my having a peaceful business was priceless. This made it easier for me to stand behind my "We aren't the right fit for what you are looking for." Also, I was aware that the emotional outbursts from these clients were the last ones I'd have with them and that made it much easier to remain detached! I can survive anything if I know it has an ending.

4. **I realized the truth of 'one door closing is another one opening.'** As I weeded out my Bad Clients, an amazing thing happened: I began to make even more money than when I'd had the Bad Clients...and with less stress.

Within a couple of weeks of letting the Bad Clients go, new Good Clients 'magically' started calling, and because I had more energy to deal with them (since I wasn't depleted from 95% of my energy going to Bad Clients), I was quick to respond to new client calls, happy to be on the phone with those clients, and eager to take care of their pet care needs.

5. **I became vigilant about not taking on any new Bad Clients.** I developed an 'intuitive ear' for new Bad Clients. I can hear them coming from a mile away now! I can hear the whine in their voice, and I really listen to the red flags that come up: When they say they've gone through five pet sitters and haven't been happy with anyone. This is not the kind of new client I want.

   I realize that due to my resolve not to take on Bad Clients, I occasionally may let some potential Good Clients slip through my fingers, but I tell you what: I'd rather let that happen than take on another draining Bad Client.

I wish you courage in letting Bad Clients go and having 100% of your energy be used toward caring for your Good Clients.

Dealing with Angry Clients

Despite providing the best customer service, there will be times when you need to deal with angry clients. I have five steps that will help you turn angry clients into happy puppies:

1. **Remember: Properly dealing with an angry client provides you the opportunity to create an even better relationship than you had with this client before they became angry.** Having that intention while resolving the situation will help you keep the goal of connection rather than dissention with the client. Everyone makes mistakes; it's how you correct the mistake and smooth your client's ruffled feathers that makes all the difference and can truly turn an angry client into a happy and loyal customer for life.

2. **If you are on the phone, let the client have her screaming fit.** She needs to get it out of her system. If you interrupt her in midstream – she will lash out at YOU, and you don't want that.

Imagine this client as an angry dog rather than a human yelling at you. If you are a pet sitter who is around dogs all the time, you probably realize that most angry dogs need to express their anger by snarling and baring their teeth. Once they've had their say, they will often just turn around and be on their merry way. But if you interrupt them by talking "Nice doggy" or stepping forward, most will attack. Both of these actions (talking or your moving forward sooner than the dog is ready) interrupt the dog's process to express his anger. People are the same.

Words to live by when dealing with an aggressive dog and client conflict: *Be still. Listen. Don't interrupt.*

3. **If the client has e-mailed you an angry e-mail, DO NOT e-mail back.** E-mail only to find a time to meet in person or talk on the phone about the issue. One of the best business tips I ever received (it's invaluable for personal relationships too) is not to discuss any difficult issues via e-mail. Take the issue to the phone or in person. Communicating a difficult subject via e-mail creates a wall between you and the other person. When walls are up, communication is difficult, if not impossible. E-mails do not afford the opportunity for non-verbal communication and voice inflection, and a lack of that can quickly lead to a misunderstanding that may make the initial problem even worse.

4. **When the client is done spewing, let them know you heard what they said and you will do whatever it takes to rectify the problem.** How do you know when they are done? Count for five LONG seconds.

If she has not spoken during the entire five seconds, it is okay for you to talk. Let her know that you are so sorry, you have heard her complaints and you completely understand how she could feel that way. (People want to be heard and not made wrong. Give them that gift and most clients will be forever grateful.)

Offer a refund. If one of your sitters did a lousy job or broke something, ask your staff member if he or she will pay for the mistake. If you feel that you are to blame because you weren't clear with your staff, own that mistake and be willing to apologize to your client verbally and offer a monetary refund.

5. **After you've offered money back, ask the client if they need anything else by saying: "I'm truly sorry about this. Is there anything else I can do to make this right?"** And be willing to do it.

Raising Rates (or How to make $4,800 more a year without doing more work!)

RAISING TEN DOG WALKING CLIENTS $2 PER WALK CAN RESULT IN $4,800 MORE A YEAR!

Let me guess: You've been thinking about raising your rates, but *thinking* about it is as far as you've gotten. This can be a costly mistake in business. Why? Well, most of your creditors raise their rates yearly to keep up with inflation. If you are not at least keeping up with the rising cost of doing business, then you are headed for financial and physical burnout because you will have to work longer hours this year to make as much as you made last year.

If it's been over a year since you've last increased your rates, here are four words of advice to help you over the rate increase hurdle:

Raise your rates yearly.

I know. Asking for a raise is hard. A lot of us experience fear that our clients will leave when we raise our rates or at the very least that our clients will give us a hard time about it. This rarely happens. Most clients will see your rate increase as a reflection that you respect yourself and your business by charging what your time is worth.

That said, raising your rates is worth any resistance you may have about taking action and actually doing it. Trust me.

Let me share with you a secret that may actually cause you to get excited about raising your rates: Let's suppose that you have ten Monday-Friday dog walking clients. It's been at least a year since you've raised their rates (using the 'raise your rates yearly' rule above), so you decide to raise your rates. Most pet sitters will raise their rates $1 or $2 per year. (Since rates and rate increases vary across the country, only you will know what will be the best rate increase for your existing clients.)

Let's say you raise your ten dog walk clients $2 per walk:

That's $10 per week MORE per client.

That's $40 per month MORE per client.

That's $100 per week MORE for all 10 clients.

That's $400 per month MORE for all 10 clients.

And yes, you guessed it...

That's $4,800 per year MORE simply for raising the rates of ten dog walking clients $2 per walk.

All for nothing! No extra dog walking, no extra marketing, no nothing. Well, not nothing...you had the *courage* to raise your rates! If you don't raise your rates, you have to get *an additional client who you charge* $400 per month for 12 months in order to make that!

That involves more WORK! So when you are feeling scared about raising prices, think about that. Better to be scared to raise prices than to have to work harder each year. Working harder each year is scarier than raising prices.

Not raising prices *will* result in burnout. Guaranteed. When we are *not* charging what our time is worth, a part of our spirit withers and gives up. We may start to think, 'What's the point of running a pet sitting business? I'm not making any money.'

Well, it may be because you haven't raised your rates for two or three years. You cannot make a decent profit if you don't raise your rates yearly or at least every other year (unless your rates are higher than average to begin with).

All that stands in the way of raising rates is fear.

In my own life, I've found that my level of self-worth usually translates to my net worth. When we raise our rates, our self-worth increases just like raises increase our net worth. Our raised self-worth causes a ripple effect of goodness which reverberates all over our lives – not just in our businesses.

Here are some tips for raising rates:

- Don't raise rates more than once a year.

- Give clients at least a month's notice.

- Raise $1 per visit or walk minimum per year. Your clients can handle a $1 raise in rate!

Raising rates is important to your staff as well. If your staff is getting paid a fair rate, they will want to continue working with you. When you raise your prices, raise your staff pay too.

Now that you understand the importance of raising your rates annually, it's time to write and send the perfect rate increase letter to your pet sitting clients. Since I just showed you how raising your rates by $2 per walk for ten clients boosts your earnings $4,800 per year, it's time to actually do it.

Below are five tips regarding writing and sending the perfect rate increase letter for your pet sitting clients:

1. **Composing a rate increase letter: Above all, keep it simple.** Do not apologize in any way, shape or form about raising your rates. Here's a sample of the rate increase letter that I send out to my own pet sitting and dog walking clients each year:

Dear Wonderful Dog Walking Clients (or Pet Sitting Clients),

It's been such a pleasure to work with you and your pets this year. Thanks so much for the opportunity of letting us care for your pets.

Due to the rising cost of doing business, we will be raising our rates slightly this year. Our rates will go up $2 per walk and $2 per pet sitting visit. Our overnight sitting rates will go up $5 per night.

As always, we are committed to providing you with excellent pet care service and we look forward to doing that for you this year.

Thanks for letting us serve you and your pets.

2. **When and how to send your rate increase letter: If you regularly mail or e-mail your dog walking or pet sitting bills simply include the rate increase letter in your next round of bills.** To make certain everyone is aware of your rate increase, you can gather the e-mail addresses of your clients and send out a mass e-mail to your business e-mail list. If you are a smaller company and deal with clients predominantly on the phone, rather than e-mail or mailing them bills, verbally tell them. However, due to the fear that may arise in declaring your rate increase, it's sometimes easier to write a letter or e-mail.

   If this is your first time raising your rates, I encourage you to take the easier route and write your clients a letter or e-mail. Don't make it harder on yourself than you need to and do remember to give each client at least a month's notice before the increase takes effect.

3. **If you are afraid that they won't want to work with you anymore, read this: I'll bet that they won't leave you if you raise your rates a dollar or two.** Why? *They are used to working with you. They like you. You like them. Their pets like you. You know the house.* Just one of the above would keep them wanting to use you no matter what you charge. Let me tell you a little secret: No one likes change. Most people don't want to search for a new pet sitter or dog walker when they can keep you and pay you a little bit more. Finding a new pet sitter is a hassle. Staying with you is

easy. And they like working with you. And remember, they don't like change (and nor do you, which is why it's hard to let your clients know you are raising your fees - even positive change can be hard for us humans).

4. **If they do leave: I know, I just said that they probably wouldn't leave but be prepared that one or two clients might.** But, hey, out of 30 or 50 or 100 clients, one or two isn't bad. And really: Do you want to work with clients who are unhappy that you are simply charging what your time is worth? I don't think so. My experience has been that the clients who leave when I've raised my rates have been clients I'd secretly wanted to let go of anyway.

Here's another secret I've learned in my years of pet sitting: After a client has left simply due to a rate increase, I've often had well-paying and enjoyable clients fill their slot soon after. Having had this experience repeated during the years I've owned my pet sitting business has helped me believe in the power of raising rates! I now let those who do want to leave, leave. And I let them go gracefully and gratefully because I know their departure makes room for clients to show up who will respect me and respect my rates.

5. **Write your own rate increase letter: Now.** It's great to read about this but you won't make any more money unless you actually write and send your own rate increase letter. I encourage you to write your own rate increase letter today and send it out to your clients tonight or tomorrow. If you love what you are doing, then you are meant to thrive financially, and this is one simple way that you can easily and effortlessly make more money this year. So what are you waiting for? Stop reading this and begin writing your own rate increase letter now then come back to this section and read on....

The Importance of Client Contracts

What does your contract include? Does it have your cancellation policy clearly stated on it? If not, you are already losing money or going to lose money in the near future. I work with a lot of pet sitters who have contracts but forget to have their clients sign them. I've been guilty of that myself, at times, especially with last-minute new clients.

> **SIX-FIGURE SUCCESS TIP**
>
> It's very important to customize your service contract to suit your business needs as situations arise in your business that demand a customized contract. Each pet sitting service business is unique, and thus, your contract will be completely different than another pet sitting company's contract. Don't be afraid to add to your contract!

Here's the thing: If you don't have clients sign the contract, you cannot enforce it. And not having an enforceable contract can be a costly mistake because you lose any rights to protect your business or to enforce your cancellation policy should they cancel last minute.

It's a good idea to remind clients of your cancellation policy even if they have signed your contract. Verbalizing your cancellation policy will also make it easier to keep a good relationship with clients. They will be more likely to honor your cancellation policy if you have verbally reviewed it with them.

Fear of Disappointment

Let go of your fear of disappointing clients if you want to catapult your pet sitting business to a six-figure one. I hear so many pet sitters say,

- "I'm afraid of disappointing my clients."
- "If I say no this time they will go with another pet sitter."
- "If I hire someone to help, they'll be disappointed that it's not me."

Actually what will disappoint them will be if you get so burned out that you go out of business! (And that will be disappointing to you too!) When we are afraid of disappointing clients, we tend to choose money and stress over peace of mind. Choose peace of mind, and you'll probably find you'll make more money. Trust me; I did.

Passing the Leash: Introducing New Staff to Clients

I think we can agree that nobody really likes change – especially when things are good. I'm sure you have clients who think the world of you and love the service you provide. Great! You're on your way to building a six-figure pet sitting business. But we've already agreed that you can't do it by yourself, and the day will come when you have to turn over clients to your staff members.

Here are five suggestions for making the transition easier on everyone:

1. **Share the jobs for a while with your new staff.** If you are hiring dog walkers, continue walking on M/W/F and have your new walker walk on T/TH.

2. **Go to at least three of the client interviews when your staff meets your clients.** After that, staff members should be able to go on their own.

3. **When clients call about particular sits and you plan to use new staff members say, "I'd love to help you, but unfortunately I'm not available for those dates. I have a wonderful assistant who is. Would you like me to set up a time to have you meet my assistant?"** If you are sharing the job say, "I'm available for some of those dates. For the dates I'm not available, I have a wonderful assistant."

4. **Have your clients pay you via mailing their checks or giving you their credit card information.** Don't have them leave checks for your staff members to pick up. It creates more work for your staff member.

5. **Don't forget to mail the client questionnaire, and be sure to include a self-addressed stamped envelope to improve the likelihood of a response.**

As I mentioned in the last chapter, a client questionnaire is an ideal way to get feedback from your clients. It also helps smooth the transition from you to a new staff member or from one staff member to a different one. It will provide you with clear information regarding whether your staff members are doing a good job with that particular client or not.

Action Step

Notice how kind you are (or are not) to your clients this week. If you are finding customer service challenging, then write yourself a note to simply:

BE KIND

In a certain sense, every client we get is a miracle. Why does our phone ring? Remember "Field of Dreams"? It's quite a bit like that in that: "If you build it, they will come." We build a website and do some marketing and clients find us. It's pretty amazing, actually. Cultivate gratitude and appreciate the miracle of getting clients if you find yourself getting crabby with them.

Action Step

Being kind is not being a doormat. Notice how you are training your clients to treat you (good and bad). Notice what is working and what is not working. Begin to set boundaries with clients in the areas that are causing you stress.

Action Step

Pay attention to any clients who are ultra-difficult to work with. Notice for a month or two how working with them does or doesn't work for you. Notice the effect these difficult clients are having on your mood. Be willing to let the difficult client(s) go if you find you are thinking about them a lot, and if they are taking your energy away from the majority of your existing clients.

Action Step

If it has been a year or longer since you last raised your rates, then it's time to do it again. Give clients a month's notice and use the model of the rate increase letter in this chapter to write your own rate increase letter. Realize that everyone feels fear in raising their rates. Feel the fear and do it anyway. You are worth it, your business is worth it and your staff is worth it.

Action Step

Begin to get rigorous about having clients sign your contract. Failure to do so often results in a loss of money and protection for your business.

THIRTEEN

Happy Holidays:

How to Have a Successful and Stress-free Pet Sitting Holiday Season

"You are surrounded by simple, obvious solutions that can dramatically increase your income, power, influence and success. The problem is, you just don't see them."

–Jay Abraham

The holidays are times of joy… and times of stress… for a lot of pet sitting business owners.

The first thing to do is to decide what your goals are for the holiday season: Time off? Lots of money? Both? Decide this first before taking any action. Think of it this way: Deciding is buying the plane ticket; taking action is getting on the plane and going.

Take a few minutes to sit and daydream about what you want out of the holiday season.

Decide:

- Which holidays really matter to you.

- What *you* do/don't want to do (i.e. visits, overnights, phone calls).

- How many visits you can/want to do.

Create:

- Spending plan: Know what's going out and coming in so you can plan your time off.

- Revenue Plan: Know what's coming in and how much you need to make during November and December (and other months) from your various revenue streams.

Sample Spending Plan

Creating a spending plan for your business will help you see how much is coming in versus how much is going out each week and each month. This will help you determine if you are on track (or over) on your spending, and during holiday periods, it will also be invaluable in determining how much you need to bring in each month in order to create a revenue plan (see the following page). It will also help you gain financial clarity regarding whether you can take time off over the holidays or not. Weekly tracking of your numbers is the most effective way to create and use a spending plan.

Here's a sample of a spending plan. You will want to add all categories that apply to your business and enter the amount you spend each week on those particular categories:

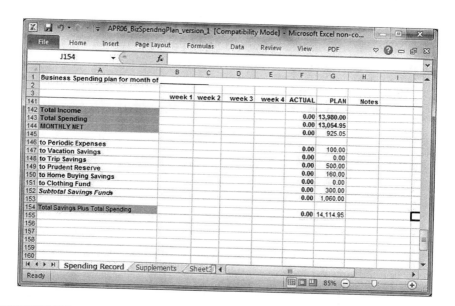

Screenshot 1:

APR06_BizSpendngPlan_version_1 [Compatibility Mode] - Microsoft Excel non-com...

File | Home | Insert | Page Layout | Formulas | Data | Review | View | PDF

J154

	A	B	C	D	E	F	G	H	I	J
1	Business Spending plan for month of									
2										
3										
		week 1	week 2	week 3	week 4	ACTUAL	PLAN	Notes		
69	Professional Services									
70	Accountant									
71	Janitorial					0.00	50.00			
72	Business Consulting					0.00	55.00			
73	Subtotal Professional Services					0.00	330.00			
74						0.00	435.00			
75	Banking Fees									
76	Checking Account Fees						0.00			
77	VISA/Mastercard Merchant fee					0.00	20.00			
78	Subtotal Banking and VISA fees					0.00	25.00			
79						0.00	45.00			
80	Office Supplies/Furniture									
81	Office supplies									
82	Table, Chairs, Furniture					0.00	215.00			
83	Subtotal Office Supplies / Furniture					0.00	0.00			
84						0.00	215.00			
85	Contracted Work									
86	Contracted work									
87	Contracted Work Subtotal					0.00	5,500.00			
88						0.00	5,500.00			
89	Business License, Insurance									
90	City Business License									
91	Trademark Fees					0.00	5.00			
92	Business Insurance					0.00	0.00			
93	Bonding					0.00	50.00			
94	Other fees?					0.00	7.00			
95	Subtotal Business Fees					0.00	0.00			
96						0.00	62.00			
97	Advertising									
98	Humane Society Newsletter									
99	Advertising-Help Wanted					0.00	15.00			
100	Advertising-Business Coaching					0.00	75.00			
101	Advertising-Website					0.00	40.00			
102	Advertising-Yellow Pages					0.00	45.00			
103	Advertising-Other					0.00	315.00			
104	Subtotal Advertising					0.00	0.00			
105						0.00	490.00			

Spending Record | Supplements | Sheet3

Ready — 85%

Screenshot 2:

APR06_BizSpendngPlan_version_1 [Compatibility Mode] - Microsoft Excel non-co...

File | Home | Insert | Page Layout | Formulas | Data | Review | View | PDF

J154

	A	B	C	D	E	F	G	H	I
1	Business Spending plan for month of								
2									
3									
		week 1	week 2	week 3	week 4	ACTUAL	PLAN	Notes	
141									
142	Total Income					0.00	13,980.00		
143	Total Spending					0.00	13,054.95		
144	MONTHLY NET					0.00	925.05		
145									
146	to Periodic Expenses								
147	to Vacation Savings					0.00	100.00		
148	to Trip Savings					0.00	0.00		
149	to Prudent Reserve					0.00	500.00		
150	to Home Buying Savings					0.00	160.00		
151	to Clothing Fund					0.00	0.00		
152	Subtotal Savings Funds					0.00	300.00		
153						0.00	1,060.00		
154	Total Savings Plus Total Spending								
155						0.00	14,114.95		
156									
157									
158									
159									
160									

Spending Record | Supplements | Sheet3

Ready — 85%

Sample Revenue Plan

Revenue plans are simple. You want to determine how much revenue you need to generate per week or per month and how you will get to that revenue.

Let's say you need to make $400 PROFIT from cat visits for December. At $20 per visit that means it will take 20 visits total in December to make your goal. 20 visits x $20 = $400.

> ### SIX-FIGURE SUCCESS TIP
>
> As I mentioned in Chapter 8: "Show me the Money", having clarity about your financial picture will help you become an empowered business owner. I'm an advocate for creating as many spreadsheets as you need to which will take you out of financial vagueness and into financial abundance. Gaining clarity about your finances creates a container for more to arrive. I've seen it over and over in my own life as well as with the coaching clients I work with. Once you create your spreadsheets (or hire someone to help you create them) you can easily insert the numbers each month and get a clear picture of the financial health of your business.

If you pay out $10 per visit to staff and you charge $20 per visit, then you need to have 40 visits to meet your goal of $400 PROFIT. 40 visits x $20 = $800 ($400 profit for you).

How to Take Time off during the Holidays

PLANNING IS THE KEY TO HOLIDAY RELAXATION.

If you've never taken a holiday off, start with one or two important days: Thanksgiving and Christmas or Hanukah. Train your staff member to cover one or two days. If you haven't hired staff members or a manager, write down (or discuss with a friend or work with me) to get clear about what stands in the way of taking that action. Often what stands in the way is trusting and letting go. Unless you want to work like a dog, hiring is the only way for you to expand your business and earn six-figures. And if you want to take off during the holidays and still generate revenue, it's your only choice.

Begin preparing your business for the holidays in September in order to have plenty of time to get clarity about what you need to do in order to have a stress-free holiday season. Get your calendar out and write all of your holiday action steps in your calendar so you stay on track. Block off the holidays you will be taking off and be unwavering about it with your clients. If you plan to take off a specific holiday and get a client calls for the holiday, but haven't yet hired a staff member who can work that time period, you can say: "My assistant will be covering for me during that time; I'll take down your reservation and call you as it gets closer." Then begin hiring process immediately! But remember: YOU'LL have to work if you fail to follow through and hire someone!

Ideally, you should hire well before the holidays, so you can get a feel for your new staff members and allow for monitoring and client questionnaires. Begin the holiday hiring process by placing an ad on Craigslist or some other help wanted site no later than September 15th if possible.

Without staff, you'll be faced with turning people away over the holidays – people who could be become clients for years. I recommend that you hire more staff members than you think you will need during the holiday season. Be sure to specify that applicants must be able to work at least two of the three holidays (Thanksgiving, Christmas/Hanukah, New Year's) or all three, if you prefer. Also, be certain to state that it's a very part-time job with no regular hours guaranteed. Let them know how much they can realistically expect to make. Be honest and be clear. Clarity upfront helps you reap positive results when you hire staff.

If you have existing staff, ask in September about their holiday season plans and which day(s) they may want off. Some pet sitting companies have a mandatory rule about staff working two out of the three major end-of-the-year holidays. It's up to you, but whatever you decide, be clear about it well in advance.

Hiring an assistant to help you with the phones during the holidays:

If you are considering hiring an assistant to cover and return incoming calls and messages over the holidays, I suggest paying a certain amount per *shift* rather than per hour. You can determine that rate by tracking how many hours you work the phones and e-mail per day and adding an extra hour. (Remember: you are used to dealing with your clients and systems, a new assistant will not be, so it will probably take longer for her to do your job.) Typically, she'll check your business phone and e-mail from her home five to six times per day (for example: 9:00 a.m., 12:00 p.m., 3:00 p.m., 6:00 p.m., 8:30 p.m.). If you want your assistant to take on more responsibility, including setting up sits, etc., consider paying more per shift. Be sure to have her simply check messages at first to get used to client requests. Establish the day/time that you will relieve her of her shift and instruct her to only call you in a dire emergency or to have you help handle setting up last-minute sits. You have hired this person to help you get a break from the business. If she is calling you every few hours with questions you are not going to get the break you need.

> YOU'D EARN A BONUS RATE IF YOU WERE EMPLOYED AND WORKED THE HOLIDAYS. BE SURE TO PAY YOURSELF AND YOUR STAFF ONE!

Have your assistant create a phone log for you and then e-mail it to you at the end of her shift, so that you don't have to look at e-mail while you are taking time off. It's your time. Really let go.

Holiday Rates

I have two words about charging holiday rates: DO IT! I typically suggest charging an additional $5-10 per night and $2-5 per visit for the entire holiday period instead of simply the specific holiday days. I define the holiday period as Thanksgiving Day through the following Sunday (four days) and from December 24th through January 2nd. Remember that you're providing a valuable service, and if you were employed and working on holidays, you'd be earning double- or even triple-overtime. Why not pay yourself (and your staff) more during the holiday period?

I also encourage you to adopt special holiday cancellation requirements. Doubling the notification time over the holiday periods for cancellations can insure that you get plenty of notice from those that do need to cancel. Holidays are particularly busy times for pet sitters, and you have the opportunity to earn a month's worth of revenue in two weeks. It's easy to book up quickly over the holidays, and you may even have to decline requests. Every late cancellation is a request you could have taken and revenue you could have earned. Don't hesitate to extend and enforce your holiday cancellation policy.

And no holiday discounts! I repeat "No holiday discounts." Unless you *need* the business because you've only been in business for one to two years or unless the client will be away for three weeks or longer.

I recommend splitting the holiday fee with your staff. If you are charging clients an extra holiday fee of $10 per night for overnight pet sitting, pay your staff $5 extra. Staff will be more likely to work over the holiday periods if they are paid more during that time.

Here's a quick example of how charging holiday rates can greatly improve your revenue:

8 visits a day for 14 days (two week Christmas period) = 112 visits x $5/extra per visit holiday fee = $560 extra ($280 for you).

If you have staff, and your company completes 224 visits during a 14-day holiday period and you are charging your clients $5 extra per visit, you'll make $1120 extra ($560 extra for you).

Gifts for your Staff and Clients

Gifts are synonymous with the holiday season. Remember that savings account I recommended earlier in the book? Saving and planning reduces stress – especially during the holiday season.

By saving early for gifts for your staff, clients, family and friends, you won't be stressed out, either financially or emotionally, in

December. Include what you'd like to buy for yourself this holiday too. Reward yourself. You deserve it!

Consider a bonus for all of those staff members who you absolutely depend on along with nice card about what you like about them and a bonus check. Be generous! It will come back to you. You can also consider a gift card for coffee, books, or restaurants. Don't buy personal items that you think they'll like unless you are 100% sure that your staff members will like them.

In order to save for the holidays, decide how much you want to spend per staff member. Here's an example: If you have four staff members and want to give $50 to one and $25 to the other three staff members, you need to set aside $125 by Dec. 20th. Divide by that amount by the number of weeks left between now and then. That's your weekly target holiday savings amount.

Don't forget your clients over the holidays. They give you business all year. It's nice to remember them as well. Here are some tried-and-true gifts for your clients:

- Santa pictures with dogs (no cats!). Check with your local Humane Society about this service (some offer it) or rent the Santa costume and have a friend dress up and go on your daily dog walks with you.

- Clear glass candle wrapped with a picture of client's pet (or a pet that has passed on is always appreciated).

- Calendar that includes a photo of the pet... along with your logo and contact information.

- Coupon for one free visit or walk in January (include an expiration date).

Remember that not everyone celebrates Christmas. Jewish clients will be celebrating Hanukah. Non-specific holiday cards and messages will cover both.

You can also consider inexpensive presents for the pets, either in lieu of or in addition to gifts for your human clients:

- Costco features big bags of dog toys/treats (12-15 quality pet items).

- Pig ears or other yummy dog treats (Good deals on these can also be found at Costco).

- Tennis balls.

- Cat toys filled with catnip (You can typically find large-order discounts online).

Action Step

Plan now for the holidays. Determine what you want to achieve and which days you want to take off.

Action Step

Create a Spending Plan and a Revenue Plan, so you can determine how much you need to earn this holiday season which will also help you determine if you can take time off this holiday season.

Action Step

Establish a holiday rate and holiday cancellation fees. Spell these out clearly in your client contracts and enforce them verbally with clients.

Action Step

Start saving now for holiday gifts for your staff, your clients, their pet... and yourself.

FOURTEEN

Ready, Set, Goal!:

Setting Goals to Achieve Pet Sitting Business Success

> *"When you set goals something inside of you starts saying, 'Let's go, let's go,' and ceilings start to move up."*
>
> –Zig Ziglar

As I'm sitting here writing this book, I'm reflecting on just how powerful a process goal-setting has been in my business life. Writing goals each year has helped me:

- Achieve (and often surpass!) the level of income I want to create.

- Work the kind of schedule I want to work (3 to 4 days a week).

- Hire the right kind of people and the right number of people for my business.

- Run my business in an outside-the-box way that adds to my happiness, prosperity and well-being.

- Travel for extended periods of time (sometimes for up to four months at a time).

- Complete the writing of this book.

I'm not the only one who has achieved success by goal setting, nor is it a new phenomenon. In 1953, researchers surveyed Yale's graduating seniors to determine how many of them had specific, written goals for their future. The answer: three percent. Twenty years later, researchers polled the surviving members of the Class of 1953 and found that the three percent with specific, written goals had accumulated more personal financial wealth than the other 97 percent of the class *combined.*

Do you have specific, written goals for your business? If not, now is the perfect time to start. And I'll share five easy steps that will help you understand not only how to go about setting goals but the 'why's' behind the psychology of the process.

1. **State your goals in the proper tense.**

   If you set a goal to begin hiring staff members, you can state it in one of two ways: "I have three quality pet sitters" or "I will hire three quality pet sitters." Notice that one is written in the present tense and one in the future tense. The first goal is more powerful than the latter.

   Writing your goals in the present tense, as if those goals are *already happening or have already happened,* affects your subconscious mind in a positive and powerful way. The subconscious mind only operates in the "now." If you create your goals in the future tense, your subconscious will rarely support you in achieving your goals.

   The subconscious mind is a powerful force, and if it is not supporting you, it can sometimes sabotage your success (or limit success) in life. Get your subconscious in alignment with what you want to create in your business and your life this year – by writing your goals in the present tense, so your subconscious can assist you in achieving what you want to achieve.

2. **Set clear, specific and measurable goals for the year.**

   When setting an income goal, you want to be very specific about the amount. If you want to make over six-figures in your pet sitting business this year, write the specific amount you want to make: "My business grosses $110,000 and my net profit is $60,000 by December 31st" instead of writing: "I earn six-figures this year."

It's important to remember that many business owners fail to think about their net income when setting goals. Don't forget about net! A reminder: Your gross is the total amount your business generates and the net amount is the amount your business actually makes after all expenses are tallied... and subtracted. Therefore, your net is the real amount your business makes, and it is the one to focus on as your net income is the barometer that enables you to know whether or not your pet sitting business is financially supporting you.

3. **Set a date by which you will achieve your specific goal.**

Let's go to back the hiring goal, so I can demonstrate what that will look like when you write your goals. Remember: You want to state that hiring goal in the present and yet have the date by which it is due be in the future.

Here's what the hiring goal will look like as a written goal: "I am hiring three pet sitters by March 15." See that? Your goal is stated in the present (not "I will hire", but simply "I am hiring") and it has a specific date by which you are going to achieve that: "March 15."

4. **Break your goals into small steps and put those small steps in your calendar now.**

If you have the goal of hiring three pet sitters by March 15, your simple steps might be:

- My hiring paperwork is organized by February 10.
- I put an ad on Craigslist by February 15.
- I send Application Packets to potential staff members by February 25.
- I conduct face-to-face interviews between March 1- March 8.
- I complete the hiring process by March 15.

Putting small steps in your calendar now is a simple way to break down a daunting or big goal into bite-sized chunks. Bite-sized chunks make your goal attainable.

5. **Post your goals where you can see them on a daily basis.**

   This step is crucial. I've found that when I have my goals in clear view, I'm much more apt to take the steps required to achieve them.

Here's a direct example of how this reaped financial rewards for me:

I have gotten into the habit of writing my specific, measurable financial goal for each month on a sticky note and taping it to my laptop. Every time I open my laptop, I see my financial goal listed on that sticky note and I'm more apt to carry out revenue-producing activities as a result of seeing my goal every time I sit down to work.

Last year at the beginning of the year, I wrote a financial goal on a sticky note that seemed a bit far-fetched – the amount I wrote was substantially more than I'd made in all prior months; however, I decided to stretch a bit and, though I didn't make that goal for the month I'd written it, I did achieve that financial goal for all of the remaining months last year!

Then at the end of last year, I decided to really go for it. I wrote a goal for that month on my sticky note for $4,000 more than I'd ever grossed in the history of my business. And guess what?

That month I grossed $4,500 more than I'd ever earned in my business.

My reaction to this was total and utter shock even though I have the experience that setting goals works! In disbelief, I double- and then triple-checked my monthly numbers. Did I really gross $4,500 more than I'd ever grossed in all the years of running my pet sitting business?

Yes I did. And you can too.

And no, it isn't magic. When we set goals, we begin to consciously and subconsciously take the actions necessary to make goals a reality.

I've worked with many pet sitting coaching clients from around the country who are amazed at the power the simple act of setting goals has in their pet sitting businesses. Will you be one of those amazed pet sitters this year? Write out your business goals and let me know what you create in your business and your life as a direct result writing down what you want for your business and your life this year. I'd love to hear from you!

Action Step

Making This Year Your Best Year Yet

It's time to write your own goals, now that you understand the "why's" behind the process and have read most of this book and are feeling ready to implement what you've learned.

Set aside 90 minutes of undisturbed time to do these exercises below.

> ### SIX-FIGURE SUCCESS TIP
> Set a timer for 45 minutes and then reset it for another 45 minutes to keep you on track and focused during this writing exercise.

As was the case with your answers to the exercises in Chapter Four: "Because You're Worth It: How Commitment and Self-Worth lead to Net Worth," the answers to these questions below will serve as your map. They are crucial for your success. They will guide you on your journey to success.

Starting out

Pick a quiet, comfortable place away from distraction.

Tools you'll need

A journal, a pen and the willingness to discover some new things about yourself and your new or existing business.

Set the timer and close your eyes. Begin by sitting quietly for a minute to get yourself really present in your desire to set clear goals for this year. When you are ready, begin writing.

In the last year, in the following areas of my *business*, what were my specific successes and accomplishments?

Financial ⎯⎯⎯⎯⎯⎯⎯⎯⎯⎯⎯⎯⎯⎯⎯

Marketing ⎯⎯⎯⎯⎯⎯⎯⎯⎯⎯⎯⎯⎯⎯

Hiring ⎯⎯⎯⎯⎯⎯⎯⎯⎯⎯⎯⎯⎯⎯⎯

Accounting/Recordkeeping ⎯⎯⎯⎯⎯⎯⎯

Taxes ⎯⎯⎯⎯⎯⎯⎯⎯⎯⎯⎯⎯⎯⎯⎯

Customer Service ⎯⎯⎯⎯⎯⎯⎯⎯⎯⎯⎯

Promotional Materials ⎯⎯⎯⎯⎯⎯⎯⎯⎯

Commitment to the Business ⎯⎯⎯⎯⎯⎯⎯

Work schedule that works for me ⎯⎯⎯⎯⎯

Stress Level ⎯⎯⎯⎯⎯⎯⎯⎯⎯⎯⎯⎯⎯

Office Organization ⎯⎯⎯⎯⎯⎯⎯⎯⎯⎯

In the last year, in the following areas of my *personal* life, what were my specific successes and accomplishments?

Family ⎯⎯⎯⎯⎯⎯⎯⎯⎯⎯⎯⎯⎯⎯⎯

Social ⎯⎯⎯⎯⎯⎯⎯⎯⎯⎯⎯⎯⎯⎯⎯

Romantic Relationship ⎯⎯⎯⎯⎯⎯⎯⎯⎯

Mental ⎯⎯⎯⎯⎯⎯⎯⎯⎯⎯⎯⎯⎯⎯⎯

Spiritual (if appropriate for you) ⎯⎯⎯⎯⎯

Physical ⎯⎯⎯⎯⎯⎯⎯⎯⎯⎯⎯⎯⎯⎯⎯

Home _____

Personal Possessions _____

_____
_____
_____
_____
_____

In the following areas of my business, what were my biggest disappointments? Failures? Avoidances? Can I understand how/ why these happened?

Financial _____

Marketing _____

Hiring _____

Accounting/Recordkeeping _____

Taxes _____

Customer Service _____

Promotional Materials _____

Commitment to the Business _____

Work schedule that works for me _____

Stress Level _____

Office Organization _____

_____
_____
_____

In the following areas of my personal life what were my biggest disappointments? Failures? Avoidances? Can I understand how/ why these happened?

Family ———————————————————————

Social ———————————————————————

Romantic Relationship ——————————————————

Mental ———————————————————————

Spiritual (if appropriate for you) ————————————————

Physical ———————————————————————

Home ———————————————————————

Personal Possessions ——————————————————

———————————————————————————

———————————————————————————

———————————————————————————

———————————————————————————

Write a few paragraphs about how I limit myself; how I will stop this behavior; what I will replace the limiting behavior(s) with and how great it will feel to stop this limiting behavior:

———————————————————————————

———————————————————————————

———————————————————————————

———————————————————————————

———————————————————————————

———————————————————————————

———————————————————————————

———————————————————————————

———————————————————————————

What are my top five most important personal and business values and how can I live them more fully in my work and life? (honesty, dependability, love, courage, trustworthiness, etc.)

_____

_____

_____

_____

_____

_____

_____

_____

_____

_____

_____

What roles do I play in my personal/business life and what were my major accomplishments in each role in the last year? (business owner, mother, father, wife, friend, son, daughter, etc.)

_____

_____

_____

_____

_____

_____

_____

_____

_____

What were my major mistakes, failures or shortcomings in each role?

_____

What is my major desire or focus for each role in the coming year?

_____

What is my top goal for each area of my business this year? What is one thing I can do regularly that will carry me toward achieving each goal?

Top Goal: **What I can do regularly:**

Financial _____

Marketing _____

Hiring _____

Accounting/Recordkeeping _____

Taxes _____

Customer Service _____

Promotional Materials _____

Commitment to the Business _____

Work schedule that works for me _____

Stress Level _____

Office Organization _____

_____

_____

_____

_____

What are my top goals for each area of my personal life this year? What is one thing I can do regularly that will carry me toward achieving each goal?

Top Goal: **What I can do regularly:**

Family _____

Social _____

Romantic Relationship _____

Mental ──────────────────────────────

Spiritual (if appropriate for you) ──────────────

Physical ──────────────────────────────

Home ────────────────────────────────

Personal Possessions ──────────────────────

What qualities do I need to have or can I develop that will ensure that I will achieve what I most desire above? (Imagine yourself a year from now: What qualities will it take to create what you most want? Write a paragraph or two below.) Some qualities might be: courage, playfulness, commitment, etc.

What support do I need in order to create my business and personal goals? (Write a paragraph or two below. List the contacts, resources, training, information, etc. that will help you achieve your goals. Also, is there a friend you can share this with, so you can support each other as you grow your business and succeed in your goals?)

Write a couple of paragraphs or more describing what you would like to accomplish in your business a year from now. Write it in the present tense: "I am...."

_____

_____

_____

_____

_____

_____

_____

Clarify your business action plan.

Review what you would like to create in your business life. Write the steps you can take to achieve your business goals:

_____

_____

_____

_____

_____

_____

_____

_____

_____

_____

_____

_____

_____

Write a couple paragraphs (or more) describing what your fulfilling personal life will look like a year from now and how you will feel accomplishing your goals:

_____

_____

_____

_____

_____

_____

_____

_____

_____

_____

_____

_____

_____

_____

_____

_____

Clarify your personal action plan.

Review what you would like to create in your personal life. Write the steps you can take to achieve your personal goals:

_____

_____

_____

_____

_____

_____

_____

_____

_____

_____

_____

_____

_____

_____

_____

_____

_____

_____

_____

_____

_____

_____

_____

Write a couple of paragraphs (or more) describing what your fulfilling personal life will look like a year from now and how you will feel accomplishing your goals:

_____

_____

_____

_____

_____

5 Tips for Powerful Goal Setting in your Business

1. **What:** Write the new goal specifically and write it in the present (not the future) tense.

2. **Why:** Understand the reasons behind what you want to achieve.

3. **Blocks:** Look honestly at what blocks you from achieving your goal.

4. **How and What:** List all of the possible ideas that could help you achieve your goal.

5. **When:** Develop a scheduled path of action with dates.

So, let's say that my goal is to create a six-figure business:

1. **What:** "I earn $100,000 in my pet sitting business."

2. **Why:** "I want to stop worrying about money. I want to be able to buy a home. I want to feel a sense of financial freedom. I want to travel."

3. **Blocks:** "I feel burned out and the thought of working harder or investing any more energy into my business now makes me feel tired. I haven't been able to get past the $60,000 mark for three years, so I'm afraid I can't ever get to $100,000."

4. **How:** "Hiring pet sitters and dog walkers to help me; getting my website search engine optimized to bring in more clients from my website, getting my business on Twitter; signing up to be a sponsor of the pet fair that is happening on September 15."

5. **When:** Pick a 'When' for each 'How' above.

I've chosen 'hiring' to give you an example of how to schedule actions in order to achieve your goal:

- **Goal:** I am hiring 3 pet sitters and 3 dog walkers by July 15.

Scheduled path of actions to take:

1. Ad on Craigslist: June 15.

2. Send Application Packets to potential applicants: June 20.

3. Review packets from applicants: June 30.

4. Set up interviews: July 1-10.

5. Hire three pet sitters and dog walkers by July 15.

FIFTEEN

Your R&R-
Relief & Relaxation:

Cures for Pet Sitter Burnout
& Planning Time for Yourself

"The bad news is time flies.
The good news is you're the pilot."

–Michael Althsuler

Every week I coach pet sitters from around the United States and Canada who are suffering from burnout and calling me for relief. I get calls from pet sitters who are so stressed out that they're often at the end of their rope. They don't have time for their kids, their partner, their own pets and they are lacking connection in their daily lives because they are isolated due to working all of the time.

Have you noticed that life becomes meaningless if all we do is work? I can relate. In the first two years of running my pet sitting business full time, I went from working 35 to 40 hours a week to working about 110 hours a week! For a couple of years, I was working seven days a week and was crabby and exhausted all the time.

When I started my business, I would be delighted by the ringing business phone, but I soon began to cringe every time the phone rang because I was already working all the time. One more call meant even more work in my already busy work schedule.

Here is a tip and it's not rocket science: If you cringe when your phone rings with new business, it's a sure sign that you're overworked, and if you don't give yourself a break soon, burnout will lead to business failure. So how do we, as pet sitters, go from burnout to having a business (and a life) that is prosperous and spacious as well as vibrant?

I went from working in my pet sitting business seven days a week to working three days a week in the space of a year. Here are four tips that helped me do that.

1. Define how you'll spend your free time once you create it.

First of all, I had to get clear on what I would do with more time. A lot of business owners who dramatically decrease their work schedules in a short period of time often get depressed because they don't know what to do with their time. Retired people experience this, too. Maybe you've experienced that deer-in-the-headlights, lost feeling when you have plans that are suddenly canceled and you're left with free time. That's a clue that you should plan how you want to spend your free time now, so you will know what to do with your time once you create your ideal work schedule.

Having a clear understanding now on how you will spend your time will help you avoid the 'time abyss.' Relaxing and doing nothing is a choice – just be conscious that it is what you want to do.

When I went from working seven days to five days to three days a week, it was obviously a big shift for me and provided a lot of free time. For most of that first year in my new schedule, I simply relaxed: I needed triage on an emotional and physical level after working seven days a week for so long.

I'd been working way too many hours, and with my newfound time, I needed and wanted to read, watch movies, garden, hang out with my cat, and have lunch with friends. The reason I could do that without feeling the stress of too much time was simple: I clearly knew what I wanted to do before starting my new 3-day workweek schedule. Because I'd gotten clear beforehand, having so much time wasn't such a shock to my system.

2. Set office hours and KEEP them.

Some pet sitters that I coach say to me, "Well, I'm not working that much, I'm only pet sitting six hours a day." And when I ask them how many additional hours are spent in the office they say, "Oh, five or six hours a day."

My reply: "Working in the office counts as working hours – count it. And let's look at how to change your work hours, so you are not working 12 hours a day!"

If you don't have staff to monitor, then 9:00 a.m. to 6:00 p.m. are reasonable office hours. Have your office hours stated clearly on your outgoing voicemail, so clients are aware of your specific work hours. That way, they won't expect a call back at night if they've called after your office hours.

If you do have staff, you will need to check messages between the hours of about 9:00 a.m. to 9:00 p.m. to make sure morning, mid-day and evening check- in/check-out pet visits and overnights are completed.

Don't answer the phone or check and respond to business e-mail after 9:00 p.m. regardless of whether or not you have staff members. Clients will adjust to your firm work hours, and you will too. Break yourself of the habit of always being available to your clients. It's just like training a dog. Through our consistent actions, we train our clients how to treat us. If you want clients to respect your time, then you need to firmly set your time boundaries and keep them.

Turn off the ringer on your business phone at night, and turn it back on in the morning. Write a note to yourself to remind you to turn the ringer off/on until it becomes a habit. I recently had a coaching client say, "I had a pet sitting client call me at 11:00 p.m.! Can you believe it?"

Well, yeah... they assume you're working if you're answering the phone at that hour. Turn that ringer off!

3. Take the "laptop & cell phone leash" off yourself.

If you have a laptop, put it in the closet when you are not using it. I'm not kidding here. This is serious stuff. I actually put my computer to bed in the closet a lot of nights. Why? Well, you probably know what I mean when I say it tugs at me like a young child yearning for my attention. I look at it, and I'm drawn to opening it up and communing with it. My silver portable beast is named Mac, and it feels good to put him to sleep in the closet most nights. Be willing to say goodbye to your computer on your days off and at night. If I can do it, so can you. Be strong!

If you don't have a laptop, it will be a little harder (if not impossible?) to put your computer in the closet. Don't worry, there's still hope for desktop-computer owners. Simply get a pillowcase or a special piece of fabric and put it over your computer, like you would a bird you were putting to sleep at night. Covering it will help reduce its magnetic pull on you. Honestly, it will!

Regarding e-mails: Create an automated e-mail message that reads: "I'm out of the office and not checking e-mail. Please call the office at <insert your office phone number> if you need to reach us. Otherwise, I'll reply to your e-mail or call you back on <whatever day you are back in the office>."

Important tip for *truly* taking the leash off: As I mentioned in an earlier chapter, do not give out your cell phone to clients. If clients already have your cell phone, then wean them off of this by referring them back to the office number via a message on your cell phone. This way, you can be truly off when the time comes to step away. By doing this, you won't cringe every time your cell phone rings thinking it's a client calling you.

4. Let go of the addiction to busyness.

Have you noticed that people are always saying, "I'm so busy" these days? Or "I don't have any time." There is an addiction to busyness, and it's pervasive in our society. It's a popular belief that being a business owner (not to mention a successful business owner) means that you will have no time. This is only a belief, it's not true!

Here's why it's not true: YOU are the boss, and YOU get to create your schedule and the kind of life you want. Therefore, you have to get clear about what you want; otherwise, you'll be swept away by the whims of your clients. You get to decide what works for you and what doesn't. Why not create a life that supports the kind of lifestyle that you want for yourself?

There are a number of other things that, although they may seem small, will contribute to burnout. The good news: There are solutions for all of them.

Burnout Challenge #1: Your clients are often late in paying you, and you have to call multiple times to get payment.

Solution A: Get a merchant credit card machine to have control over when clients pay. PayPal is great, but clients have to take action, so you still don't have control over when you get your money. Costco has good rates for merchant credit card processing. If you are using an administration software system for your business, you can link your merchant account to your computer system so that you can process credit cards with the click of a button!

Solution B: Have clients mail a check prior to departure. Say or e-mail: "In order to ensure your reservation, we will need to receive payment three days prior to departure. A post-dated check for the final date of service is also fine." The important thing is to get full payment prior to departure.

Burnout Challenge #2: You don't know why, but you find that you often attract difficult and ultra-picky clients who are not easy to work with.

Solution: Get skilled at seeing the signs of impossible clients: "We've gone through three pet sitters this year" is a comment that is an immediate red flag. "Good" clients typically don't fire three pet sitters. Other indicators of impossible-to-please clients: Writing a novel as instructions for their pets and interrogating you during the initial phone call about where you find your people, etc. Choose NOT to take difficult people on as clients... from the start.

Burnout Challenge #3: You often have clients calling for services one to three days prior to departure, and you have to scramble to meet with them or set up a sitter to meet with them.

Solution: Charge a $30 last-minute fee. Say, "We'd love to help, and there's a lot of schedule re-arranging so that our staff member, Suzie, can meet with you, so we do charge a $30 last-minute fee for requests with less than 72 hours' notice. She's definitely available. Can I go ahead and get your information so I can set up a meeting?"

Burnout Challenge #4: You aren't making enough money by only providing pet sitting. You've done all the marketing suggestions recommended in this book and you aren't sure what to do.

Solution: Offer mid-day dog walking services for those who work. This is the one consistent service that you can offer that will be the bread and butter of your business and perhaps even the foundation of your business.

Burnout Challenge #5: You offer dog walking, and some dog walking clients stop service suddenly which puts you in a precarious financial situation.

Solution: Clearly state in your contract that you require a minimum of two weeks' notice to cancel dog walking service and that failure to do so will require that client being billed for two weeks of normal service.

Burnout Challenge #6: You are tired of answering the business phone and find yourself cringing when the phone rings.

Solution A: If you do not have a separate business phone line, get one as soon as possible! Do not give clients your cell phone number. They can call your business line. It doesn't matter if your business phone is a land line or cell phone, but have one number for business-only calls.

If you use your personal cell phone to return client calls, be sure to have your number blocked or made into a private number, so they can't use the caller ID to call you back on what you want to be your personal phone.

Solution B: Hire a phone assistant or a manager to help you manage your business. Be willing to have someone else do your job for a little while, so you can get a well-needed break. You'll come back refreshed and ready to give stellar customer service.

You Deserve a Vacation

A sure-fire way to suffer burnout in the pet sitting business is to fail to take any time off.

Are you:

- Feeling jealous when you hear your clients/friends talk about their vacations?

- Consumed by work and feeling like you don't have a life?

- Exhausted all the time?

Then it is probably time for *your* vacation. The key to being able to step away from your pet sitting business without worrying about the lack of revenue or business management is to plan properly.

Here are five steps to set up your pet sitting business, so you can go on your vacation:

1. **Plan in advance.** Choose your departure date at least two months in advance to allow yourself plenty of time to plan and coordinate the details. A last-minute decision and departure are going to lead to lost revenue and extra stress. Decide on your vacation destination and duration well in advance.

2. **If you don't have pet sitters who are working for you and you don't want to hire pet sitters, send an e-mail to your client list advising them of your vacation dates.** Add your vacation dates to your business voicemail as well. Find a local pet sitting business owner to refer your business to during your vacation. Ask that they refer you when they go on vacation, so you create a reciprocal business relationship; one that serves both of your businesses.

3. **If you have staff, map out a plan of who will do what and when.** Get your regular daily dog walks covered. When pet sitting clients call to request you for the dates that you will be gone say, "I'm not available but my wonderful assistant is. When can I set up a time to have you meet him?"

4. **Consider who, among your staff, can answer the phones and check messages while you are away, so you don't lose business opportunities.** Begin training them now, and assign your staff shifts before you depart, so that they are amply prepared to manage while you're away.

5. **Begin saving money for your vacation.** Set up a specific savings account just for your trip and begin to siphon money into it, so that you are able to have an abundant trip. Get in the habit of adding to this savings account on a monthly basis, so that your next trip will be financially feasible.

ENJOY your trip!

Action Step

Avoid burnout by defining how you'll spend your free time, setting and sticking to your office hours, unleashing yourself from your computer and cell phone, and breaking the "busyness" addiction.

Action Step

Remember there is at least one solution to the little challenges that can pile up and lead to burnout. Take one today!

Action Step

Take the steps necessary in order to take a vacation. No matter where you go or what you do, it's imperative to take some time away from your business.

SIXTEEN

The End:

(But not really...)

*"A business has to be involving, it has to be fun,
and it has to exercise your creative instincts."*

–Richard Branson,
British Virgin Group Founder

It's the end of this book and by now, if you've done or been doing the exercises I've laid out in this book, you have probably seen a dramatic jump in your income (both gross revenue and the all-important net profit). And if you haven't done the exercises, I recommend that you go back and do them. Doing the exercises is a declaration to your subconscious, yourself, and to your business that you are willing to do what it takes to make the kind of profit that you deserve to make in your business.

I'm committed to you earning six-figures in your pet sitting business this year. But the real question is:

Are YOU committed to earning six-figures in your business this year?

Making six-figures in your business is really only the beginning. After you are making the kind of profit you need and want to make in your business, you can then tweak your business to become whatever it is *you* want it to be.

Do you want to work three days a week? *You can do it.*

Do you want to travel around the world for six months while having a trusted manager run your pet sitting business while you are away? *You can do it.*

Do you want to spend more time with your kids and spouse and relax and do fun things on a daily basis while your business essentially runs itself (with the help of your manager)? *You can do it.*

Running a business (especially a pet sitting business) is a never-ending adventure. Running a business is a creative process... anything is possible. The only limits that are on your business are the ones you place on it.

As I said, making money is only the beginning. What do you want to create now that you've made the money? Review the writing you did in Chapter Four: *Because You're Worth It: How Commitment and Self-Worth Lead to Net Worth.* What you wrote in that chapter will remind you why you started this journey in the first place.

Don't forget that you are the boss. You are the captain of your ship (your business). You are the map-maker, the navigator, the driver. You get to run your business in the way that works best for you.

Have fun with it!

Programs to Help you Achieve
Six-Figure Pet Sitting Business Success...Now!

Now that you know that it is possible to achieve six-figure success in your pet sitting business, you've set your sights on creating a work/life that is in alignment with what you value and cherish.

To help speed up your process, I created the following programs that provide greater support than you can get from a book alone.

Catapult! Six-Figure Pet Sitting Success Group:

This business success group is held via teleconference with pet sitters from around the country who are committed to creating and supporting each other to six-figure pet sitting business success. I facilitate this telegroup and offer it once or twice a year for pet sitters. The group meets for four sessions over a two-month period. The group is a powerful, effective tool to quickly transform your struggling business to a thriving enterprise as well as to get out of the isolation that plagues so many pet sitting business owners.

Check the SFPSA website for more details and to sign up for the next Catapult! Group:

http://www.sixfigurepetsittingacademy.com/petsitter_business.html

Private Business Coaching with Kristin Morrison:

Are you ready to take your business to the next level but need support and hand-holding to help you do that? I can help you take your business where you want it to go, quickly and easily. I've helped hundreds of pet sitting business owners from around the country, and I can definitely help you with whatever challenges you face in your pet business.

Visit my business coaching page for testimonials and to sign up for business coaching with me:

http://www.sixfigurepetsittingacademy.com/business_coaching.html

Search Engine Optimization (SEO) Coaching:

In just one complete session, I can take most pet sitting websites from low (or non-existent) on the search engines to page one.

Visit my SEO coaching page to find out more:

http://www.sixfigurepetsittingacademy.comPetSitterSearch EngineOptimization.html

I would love to hear how this book has helped you succeed in business!
E-mail me: success@sixfigurepetsittingacademy.com

Websites for Pet Sitting Business Success:
http://www.SixFigurePetSittingAcademy.com
http://www.SixFigurePetSittingBook.com

Connect with Six-Figure Pet Sitting Academy™ on these social media sites:
Facebook: www.facebook.com/SixFigurePetSitting
Twitter: @PetSittingCoach
LinkedIn: www.linkedin.com/in/sixfigurepetsitting

Recommended Resources:

FREE Pet Sitting Business Resources:

1. Visit the SFPSA Resources page for a free sample rate increase letter:

   http://www.sixfigurepetsittingacademy.com/resourcespetsitting.html

2. Sign up for the FREE Six-Figure Business Tips and Tools Newsletter:

   (Sign up box at top right of home page)

   http://www.sixfigurepetsittingacademy.com/index.html

3. Visit the Six-Figure Pet Sitting Academy™ blog for business tips, Kristin's travel and business adventures, and articles on how to create a pet sitting business and life beyond your wildest dreams!

   http://www.sixfigurepetsittingacademy.com/blog

Coach Kristin's Recommended Reading Shelf

Business Books:

Want to read more on how to create prosperity in your business? Below are some of the books that are on my bookshelf and that have been crucial to my business success.

Think and Grow Rich by Napoleon Hill
If you only read one book from this list make this the book. A timeless classic on how to create wealth with ease.

The Type-Z Guide to Success: A Lazy Person's Manifesto for Well and Fulfillment by Marc Allen
One of my favorite business books of all time. I often loan this book out to my business-owning friends but only with the clear instruction that I must have it back when they are finished with it. This is the only book that I read multiple times a year and it affirms my belief that making money can be easy and fun. Marc Allen is also an inspiring public speaker, and he's so lazy that when he speaks, he speaks from a Lazy Boy chair!

Attracting Perfect Customers by Stacey Hall and Jan Brogniez
This book helps clarify what your Ideal Client is and how to create a client base of your Ideal Clients. A must for pet sitters who want clients who are easy and fun to work with!

Sabbath: Restoring the Sacred Rhythm of Rest by Wayne Mueller
Oh, I adore this book. When I'm feeling frazzled and need to relax this book instantly calms me down with its short, soothing chapters. It's a great book to read before bed.

It also offers gentle reminders of what really matters most in this life and helps get me back on my right life track when I've slipped off.

Secrets of Six-Figure Women by **Barbara Stanny**
I have and will continue to highly recommend this book to many of my pet sitting coaching clients (both men and women) who are struggling with breaking through the self-imposed glass ceiling of six-figures.

Overcoming Underearning by **Barbara Stanny**
If you find yourself having a hard time asking clients for a raise or are consistently offering discounts, this book is for you.

Earn What You Deserve by **Jerrold Mundis**
This book is an easy, quick read and contains powerful information about how to thrive financially.

The Diamond Cutter: The Buddha on Managing Your Business and Your Life by **Geshe Michael Roach**
If you want to incorporate spirituality into your finances, this book is for you. Here's what one Amazon reviewer had to say about this book: "A cross between the Dalai Lama's Ethics and Stephen Covey's '7 Habits' book, The Diamond Cutter will have you gardening a path to the bank."

Web Copy that Sells by **Maria Veloso**
If you are looking to create a pet sitting website that is a powerful vehicle for client calls and sales, you'll find this book helpful. Learn what makes your customers want to call or e-mail you and how you can incorporate "call to action" words and images on your site in order to get clients to do business with you!

50 Powerful Ideas You Can Use to Keep Your Customers by **Paul R. Timm, Ph.D.**
I didn't expect to find new customer service ideas in this book, but I did. Short, simple ideas to keep your customers happy (which will keep you happy).

The Artist's Way by **Julia Cameron**
As I mentioned in Chapter 5, this powerful book has been influential in cultivating my creative side (an often over-looked skill in business) as well as helping me get to the heart of why I want money (freedom to be with the people I love and to have plenty of time to do the things I love to do including travel for extended periods of time).

About the Author

Kristin Morrison is a pet sitting business owner, business coach and guide for pet business owners. Kristin is the founder of the Six-Figure Pet Sitting Academy™. Through pet sitting business ownership, writing, and helping pet sitters run successful, empowered pet businesses, Kristin has found her Right Livelihood.

Kristin lives part of the year in Bali and part of the year in California. When she is in Bali, Kristin is committed to living her life mostly unleashed from her business. If you contact her while she's in Bali, her assistant will let you know when Kristin will be back and taking on coaching clients again. New coaching clients are always welcome, and Kristin will be sure to fit you in when she returns!

CPSIA information can be obtained at www.ICGtesting.com
Printed in the USA
LVOW090946271011

252162LV00003B/417/P